Dealing with Diversity through Multicultural Fiction

Library-Classroom Partnerships

LAURI JOHNSON AND SALLY SMITH

American Library Association / Chicago and London 1993

School Media Centers: Focus on Trends and Issues

CULTURAL PLURALISM AND CHILDREN'S MEDIA by Ester Dyer

PROJECTING A POSITIVE IMAGE THROUGH PUBLIC RELATIONS by Cosette Kies

A STUDY OF COMBINED SCHOOL-PUBLIC LIBRARIES by Shirley Aaron

INSTRUCTIONAL DESIGN AND THE LIBRARY MEDIA SPECIALIST by Margaret E. Chisholm and Donald P. Ely

continued by

School Library Media Programs: Focus on Trends and Issues, edited by Eleanor Kulleseid

THE INSTRUCTIONAL CONSULTANT ROLE OF THE SCHOOL LIBRARY MEDIA SPECIALIST by Betty P. Cleaver and William D. Taylor

AT THE PIRATE ACADEMY by Gary Zingher

DESIGNING AND RENOVATING SCHOOL LIBRARY MEDIA CENTERS by Jane D. Klasing

DEALING WITH DIVERSITY THROUGH MULTICULTURAL FICTION by Lauri Johnson and Sally Smith

Photo Credits

Photo on cover and page 34 courtesy of Vashti Davidson-Clark.
Photos on pages 70 and 78 courtesy of Murray Nobelman.
Photos on pages 7, 18, 27, 51, and 85 by the authors.

Library of Congress Cataloging-in-Publication Data
Johnson, Lauri
    Dealing with diversity through multicultural fiction : library-
classroom partnerships / by Lauri Johnson & Sally Smith.
      p. cm. — (School library media programs. Focus on trends and
issues ; no. 12)
    Includes bibliographical references.
    ISBN 0-8389-0605-2
    1. Intercultural education—New York (N.Y.) 2. Pluralism (Social
sciences) in literature. 3. School libraries—New York (N.Y.) —
Activity programs. I. Smith, Sally 1944– . II. Title.
III. Series.
LC1099.4.N7J64 1993
370.19′ 6—dc20   92-38872
                                      CIP

Printed in the United States of America.

97 96 95 94   5 4 3 2

Contents

Acknowledgments

We gratefully acknowledge Geraldine Clark for her vision, guidance, and support in the early years of our program, and Betty Kulleseid who understood that this book needed to be written and showed us the way.

Grateful thanks also go to David Roberson and Bob Weiss for their constant support and belief in our work, and to Carol Wreszin whose critical response was essential to the continued growth of Project Equal.

This book would not have been possible without the teachers, librarians, and students of New York City from whom we learned so much. Thanks!

Introduction

The concept of cultural diversity, one of the great themes of the modern era, has evolved continuously throughout a century of global turbulence. In the United States the civil rights movement has given it a constructive turn. A once prevalent assumption of minority perspectives as sanctioned within the mainstream culture is yielding to a more fluid and comprehensive concept of many cultures and lifestyles linked by needs, behaviors, and institutions common to all human beings.

Dealing with Diversity through Multicultural Fiction is an effort to come to terms with the complexities involved in such profound social change. Here the reader will encounter a learning community of teachers and students who are trying to understand themselves and others through reading, reflection, discussion, and an exploration of values and attitudes. These attitudes are defined in relation to personal and group identity, as well as to awareness of cultural, ethnic, physical, and other differences. Real-life issues of stereotyping and prejudice are confronted through encounters with fictional characters in realistic young adult novels. The goal is to develop tolerance, an acceptance of others who are different from self and family, and beyond that, to foster empathy, the ability to put oneself in another's shoes because one recognizes and shares the feelings and circumstances of that person.

A number of characteristics distinguish this book from numerous others devoted to the subject of multicultural education. One is the demonstration of powerful partnerships among library media specialists, reading specialists, and classroom teachers at school, district, and central board levels within a large urban school system. Geraldine Clark, Director of the Library Unit of the New York City Board of Education from 1976 to her retirement in 1989, was a prime mover in setting up a model curriculum with the authors, both reading specialists, as coordinators. She saw this as a challenge and opportunity for students and teachers alike. Although New York and other states espouse the concept of integrating library and information skills into the curriculum, she noted that "In practical situations library media specialists and classroom teachers frequently have difficulty translating this ideal into curriculum. In addition, library media specialists tend to resist actively pursuing their role as instructional consultants."

As a former young adult librarian, Ms. Clark recognized that quality contemporary literature for young adolescents was common ground upon which teachers and library media specialists could build complementary learning experiences. Her vision and tenacity were in no small part responsible for the development and success of the project upon which *Dealing with Diversity* is based—a model for cooperative endeavor that is nothing less than a collective call to action.

Another special characteristic is the demonstrated longevity and success of this model, based on Project Equal, an externally funded program in New York City that became institutionalized and self-supporting. The program has continued to flourish, even during periods of political and economic instability, not only because it is educationally sound but also because it offers a vehicle for middle school students to address challenging social and personal issues. During the 1992–93 school year more school districts applied for participation than available staff could handle, and clients had to be turned away. Program strength was further demonstrated when project leaders and participants were able to finesse an intellectual freeedom challenge that, under other circumstances, could have compromised or even destroyed the program. Such resiliency speaks to the successful collaborative process among the participants in schools that implemented Project Equal. It also speaks to the recognition by educators that such programs are desperately needed.

A third important characteristic is the program's interdisciplinary and nontraditional content. Two separate but interdependent sequences of activities have an explicit curricular base in language arts, with a strong reading and literature component. The program also has an implicit curricular base in the social studies, with strong values clarification and citizenship components. Concepts and methods drawn from both curriculum areas are innovative and developmentally oriented; they will be familiar to educators who espouse such approaches as literature-based curriculum, whole language, and cooperative learning. They offer alternative teaching/learning strategies that can co-exist with traditional whole group classroom instruction.

A final significant characteristic of *Dealing with Diversity* is the inclusiveness of the curriculum model presented. This is based, to some extent, upon the evolution of Project Equal. Participants gradually expanded both the mission and the definition of multiculturalism throughout its first decade of existence. To the original study of differences in gender, age or generation, family structure, and disabilities were added differences in ethnicity, race, and culture. This expansion was a response to a perceived need for it in the schools.

Inclusiveness refers to audience as well as to content. This multicultural curriculum can be adapted to any school environment, regardless of geography or demographics. It will be useful to professionals teaching in suburban, small town, and rural communities as well as in big cities. Furthermore, it can be implemented with students at any level from sixth through twelfth grade. The job can only be done, however, with the leadership of educators who are willing to acknowledge and confront the differences that make for misunderstanding, anxiety, and downright conflict in their own local communities. Those who adapt the strategies and content to specific situations will discover that dealing with diversity can be a risky enterprise. By exploring students' attitudes and behaviors, as well as those of characters in good fiction, educators will need to come to terms with their own attitudes and prejudices. As the following pages will attest, the rewards are well worth the risks.

ELEANOR R. KULLESEID
Series Editor

1

Project Equal: Creating Empathy and Equity

Project Equal is a program to educate children about prejudice and stereotyping. We read and discuss books in groups about kids that face problems. Project Equal teaches us how to handle tough situations. Hopefully we'll make the right decisions. Sometimes our friends are doing something that is wrong but we can't go along with the crowd. We have to stand up and stick to what we believe in. Project Equal taught us about life, values, courage, and most importantly, human respect.

Theresa Inga
Fifth Grade Student [1]

It was a fifth grade class in a predominantly Italian American neighborhood in Brooklyn. The school was tightly knit, with almost a "small town" feeling about it. The neighborhood was beginning to change, however. Asian immigrants were moving in, starting new businesses, and the district was faced with increasing numbers of children coming to school who didn't speak English. A small number of African American students were bused into the school from a nearby neighborhood. A series of incidents of racial violence the previous year had rocked New York City, polarizing neighborhoods, especially in Brooklyn. The students had seen the news reports, heard their parents' views, and were confused and somewhat hesitant to talk about the disturbing events. Was school the place to discuss these sensitive social issues? When state and local curricular mandates already demanded so much attention, was there even time to address these concerns in class?

The teacher and the library media specialist at this school were able to answer "yes" to these questions and confront the situation head on because of the school's participation in Project Equal, a multicultural literature-based program that integrates lessons on respect and acceptance of differences into the ongoing curriculum. "Let's make prejudice and discrimination the focus of our program this year," they said. The class explored these themes with the library media specialist and teacher on a weekly basis for about six months, with regular visits by the project facilitator. Lively classroom discussions on what it means to be male and female had energized the girls and sensitized the boys, alerting both to the potentials for prejudice and discrimination based on gender. Students eagerly read multicultural novels; some completed twenty or more independently. Small group discussions in the library media center on these books had slowly yielded some honest insights. In a discussion about *Felita* (Mohr), one group talked about how they felt when someone from a different racial background moved into their neighborhood. "I probably would have been one of those girls teasing Felita, telling her to go back where she came from," one girl admitted. "Now I know how Felita felt."

It was clear that the students loved reading and discussing the novels. But did they understand stereotyping and its relation to prejudice and discrimination? Had their minds been opened to diversity, even a little? "Write about what Project Equal has meant to you," the teacher said one day in the spring. "What have you learned from this program?" Theresa and the other students wrote, with an openness and interest in fairness that is so characteristic of ten-year-olds.

Project Equal, a program for middle grade students (grades 5–8), grew out of the conviction that children can and must grapple with issues of diversity and that literature provides an effective way both to better understand their own experience and to empathize with children from different backgrounds. Some multicultural programs focus on the uniqueness of specific cultures and world views, while others emphasize the commonalities in the American experience. Project Equal attempts to synthesize these approaches and help teachers, librarians, and students appreciate the differences and recognize the universals. It also explores through reading, surveys, and small group discussions the concept of stereotyping and the consequences of prejudice and discrimination based on race, ethnicity, gender, age, and disabilities. In addition, Project Equal seeks to develop critical reading skills, motivate reading for pleasure, and provide a model for library-classroom collaboration in which students, teachers, and library media specialists explore together the challenges of finding identity in a diverse society.

The Call for Multicultural Education

What is the need for such a program? Many educators may say, "Our school is homogeneous. All of our students are from the same background," or "That's an urban issue. We don't have those problems here." There is increasing evidence, however, that the changing family patterns and demographics that have influenced urban school districts will have a greater impact on all schools in the near future, regardless of geographic location.

The Changing Face of U.S. Society

Who will be our students in the future? How will their lives be different from our own? We live in a rapidly changing society. The composition of the American family and roles within the family have responded to economic realities and new perspectives on gender roles. In 1970, 29 percent of women with preschool children worked outside the home.[2] By 1995, researchers estimate that two-thirds of all preschool children and three-fourths of all school-age children will have mothers in the work force.[3] The traditional nuclear family with a breadwinning father, homemaker mother, and two children now constitutes less than 10 percent of all families.[4] One in every two marriages in the United States ends in divorce and more than half of all children born today will live in a single-parent household at some time in their lives.[5] Other alternate family styles, such as gay families, are now being publicly acknowledged, with estimates that 6 to 14 million children are being raised by gay or lesbian parents.[6]

The racial and ethnic makeup of the country is also undergoing striking changes. The Commission on Minority Participation in Education and American Life estimates that by the year 2000 one in three Americans will be a person of color,[7] including about 40 percent of all adolescents.[8] In some states, such as California, and in large urban centers such as Chicago, Philadelphia, and Washington, D.C., the majority of public school students are children of color. Approximately 80 percent of children in the New York City Public Schools are from African American, Hispanic, Asian, or Native American backgrounds.[9] Recent immigration from the Caribbean, the former Soviet Union, the Middle East, and Asian countries has resulted in an expanding need for bilingual and E.S.L. (English as a Second Language) programs in many "gateway" cities such as Los Angeles, Miami, and New York. Some districts must accommodate a student population with forty to fifty different home languages.

Increasing racial and ethnic diversity is not limited to large urban centers. Some areas of the country, such as the Southwest, have always had substantial Hispanic and Native American populations, which are growing with continued immigration from Mexico and Central America. Even the Midwest is experiencing the effects of the new wave of immigration. For instance, the largest Hmong community of immigrants from Southeast Asia is located in the Minneapolis–St. Paul area.

Economic diversity is also a continuing issue for many public school districts. Contrary to popular belief, most severe poverty among youth is concentrated in rural areas, not in the inner cities, and is especially severe in the South.[10] Children of migrant families or those who live in isolated rural areas may attend school only sporadically because of work and family responsibilities.

Students need to be prepared for the world they will inhabit as adults. The movement toward a global community and the increasing diversity of the United States require adults who have the knowledge, understanding, and respect to live and work in this multicultural environment. Differences in culture, race, and economics are already impacting on children in urban areas. Children living in homogeneous communities will also need to understand the benefits and responsibilities of living in a diverse world.

Approaches to Multicultural Education

How are the history and experiences of children from diverse backgrounds and family styles reflected in the school's curriculum? The movement to develop and implement "education that is multicultural" is not new. Theorists and researchers such as James Banks, Carl Grant, and Christine Sleeter have been defining and redefining the issues for more than fifteen years.[11] Multicultural education, however, like other educational reform movements, has been subject to shifts in political priorities and funding realities. The new influx of immigrants, more parent and community involvement in local schools, and an increase in bias-related incidents have intensified the debate about the shape and future direction of multicultural education.

Divergent views about what constitutes an "American identity" and a struggle over who should participate in shaping the curriculum have raised central questions about the study of diversity. Is there a common American identity and heritage that was derived from a European legal system and literary tradition?[12] How do the history and cultural perspective of different racial and ethnic groups that make up U.S. society differ? What can the schools do to reduce prejudice and promote the acceptance of differences among children from different racial and ethnic groups?

Although the mass media often characterize the debate as if there were only two camps, there are important differences in approach included under the umbrella of multicultural education. Some programs provide intensive study of a single racial or ethnic group. Afrocentric programs attempt to infuse the curriculum with African American and African content and to center the African American child within the context of familiar cultural and social references from their own historical settings.[13] Other programs work to reduce prejudice through case studies of particular historical events like the Holocaust.[14] A growing number of conflict resolution programs are included as part of a multicultural curriculum, training students as mediators to resolve conflicts that arise in the classroom and on the playground.[15]

Most multicultural programs have focused on history and/or culture and have been implemented as part of the social studies curriculum. A few educators and researchers have advocated using literature as the foundation of a multicultural program, but these programs have been largely theoretical.[16] Pressure on school libraries to increase multicultural collections has resulted in more bibliographies,[17] but there is still a lack of clearly defined programs. Although there is some support among theorists and policy makers for addressing other issues of diversity, such as gender, social class, exceptionality,[18] and sexual orientation,[19] most multicultural programs in practice have been limited to a focus on race and ethnicity.

Project Equal's Inclusive Approach: Stereotyping

Project Equal takes an inclusive approach to multicultural education, developing students' understanding of the general concept of stereotyping, then applying that concept to specific examples based on race, ethnicity, gender, age, and disabilities. Students begin with awareness activities that explore their attitudes and values regarding stereotyping and the effects of prejudice and discrimination. Then they read realistic multicultural novels chosen because they highlight developmental themes that have particular importance for young adolescents in a diverse society—friendships, family relationships, racial and ethnic prejudice, and identity issues. Books that contain active older characters and children who are disabled are incorporated in a naturalistic way within the themes of friendships and family relationships. Through independent reading, discussion, and writing activities, students and teachers sharpen their awareness of diversity. Teachers and library media specialists work collaboratively to implement the program in the classroom and library.

The Literature Component: Connecting Reading and Real Life

In our growing technological world, young adolescents often obtain information and recreation from television, video games, and computer programs, not from books. A recent review of research on recreational reading reported in the *English Journal* found that 75 percent of middle school students spend less than an hour each day reading.[20] In contrast, 71 percent of eighth graders tested by the National Assessment of Educational Progress reported watching three or more hours of television a day.[21] According to Meek, television's one-dimensional characters, not complex characters from literature, become reference points for today's children.[22]

Our challenge as teachers and library media specialists is to find ways to reconnect children, especially adolescents, with literature in ways that are meaningful to them. Literature can still transport us places, touch our emotions, and fuel our imaginations in ways that no other instructional or communication medium can. Realistic fiction, in particular, can expose young adolescents to real problems they may face in their lives and help them explore viable solutions.

The Role of Books in Shaping Children's Attitudes

What is the research evidence to support the influence of literature on children's attitudes toward diversity? Despite the intuitive appeal of the notion that literature does affect the way children see the world, there have been relatively few studies that systematically examine this issue. Most researchers have pointed to racial and sex-role stereotypes in children's literature; they have concluded that stereotyped portrayals negatively influence self-concept and support a narrow and limited world view. A few studies have attempted to influence students' views toward gender roles by portraying male and female characters in nontraditional roles.[23] Others have examined the impact of reading fiction depicting the African American experience on both black and white children.[24] Different types of interventions and the lack of valid and reliable measures used across studies make it difficult to quantify the impact of literature on student attitudes.

A more promising line of research looks at student response to literature through interviews, group discussions, writing samples, and ethnographic studies. This naturalistic view of how students interact with literature often shows that the same novel or story can influence different readers in different ways, depending on their previous knowledge of both content and structure.[25] Informal classroom studies show that students respond emotionally to the characterizations and themes in books they read and are moved to discuss them with others and write about their reactions.[26] Guided group discussion can mediate and influence students' interpretations of what they have read.[27]

Since reading is such an established part of any curriculum, linking issues of equality and diversity with a literature program helps overcome discomfort and resistance to a multicultural curriculum and makes it more likely that teachers and librarians will discuss these issues with students as an integral part of the ongoing curriculum. Administrators are also more likely to support a program that meets the multiple goals of promoting acceptance of differences, motivating reading for pleasure, and providing a model of interdisciplinary cooperation.

Many educators believe that younger children will be more receptive to strategies that change attitudes than older students. Project Equal is targeted at the middle grades, however, because of the developmental readiness of ten- to fourteen-year-olds to understand issues of diversity. Young adolescents are more likely than younger children to make generalizations, to look at situations from a variety of viewpoints, and to anticipate the consequences of decisions and actions. They also have a greater ability to evaluate the sense and reality of information. These characteristics make young adolescents particularly receptive to a program that promotes the recognition and understanding of stereotypes and ensure that they will be better able to comprehend and respond to realistic fiction with more complex characterizations.

Developing Critical Reading Skills through an Awareness of Stereotyping

Some teachers and library media specialists begin their Project Equal involvement with resistance to exploring issues of diversity. "The books you use in Project Equal are so great. Why don't we just have them read the books and forget about discussing stereotyping?" In Project Equal students first develop an understanding of the concept of stereotyping through surveys and open-ended class discussions. They explore their perceptions of male and female roles, family styles, and racial and ethnic prejudice and discrimination through values clarification, role-playing, and problem-solving activities. This conceptual understanding provides an important foundation for analyzing and discussing the multicultural realistic fiction students read independently. Students who have read the same book are able to meet in small groups led by the participating teacher, library media specialist, and the project facilitator to discuss characterizations,

how problems are resolved, and students' responses to the book. Critical reading skills develop through comparing and contrasting books on themes such as peer pressure, family relationships, or racial and ethnic prejudice and discrimination. Students are encouraged to identify with characters like themselves and empathize with those who are different.

Motivating Reading for Pleasure

Project Equal supplies participating schools with multiple copies of contemporary realistic fiction to read independently at home. Books are introduced thematically through book talks by the library media specialist and/or teacher, who tell just enough about the story to interest students and leave them wanting to read more. Students can select books from those presented that interest them at their reading level. All independent reading is judged successful; the reluctant reader who completes one novel for the first time is as celebrated as the avid reader who may read more than twenty books.

A Model of Library-Classroom Collaboration

Many library media specialists will agree with the middle school librarian who said, "I'd like to work more closely with classroom teachers, but I haven't found a mechanism to do it." Project Equal provides a way for librarians and classroom teachers to work together through planning and implementing a literature-based curriculum. The flexible nature of the program allows the librarian and participating teachers from each school to decide how to implement the general goals of the program.

At the beginning of the program, project participants decide what themes and activities they want to emphasize and select relevant titles from the project list. Biweekly planning meetings ensure that planning will be ongoing and responsive to the needs of the students. Each staff member brings his or her unique perspective and skills to this library-classroom partnership. Such partnerships may also include other staff who function as facilitators, including reading specialists, social studies coordinators, school-based staff developers, or district library media supervisors.

History

The genesis of Project Equal was work carried out by researchers, activists, and organizations like the Council for Interracial Books for Children to document the presence of racial and sex-role stereotypes in juvenile fiction and their negative effect on children.[28] Nancy Larrick's 1965 survey, reported in "The All White World of Children's Books," documented the exclusion of African American characters and the negative images and stereotypes presented when black characters did appear.[29] Larrick's survey was followed by Broderick's comprehensive look at the black image in children's books from the 1800s until 1970.[30]

The portrayal of girls and women in children's books also came under fire in the 1970s. Weitzman's classic study of picture books pointed out that girls often were depicted as quiet, inactive, and willing to let others solve their problems for them.[31] This initial study was followed by examinations every few years of award-winning children's books to see if the portrayals had changed over time.[32]

Sharon Wigutoff and Jeanne Bracken, editors at The Feminist Press, a non-profit group dedicated to publishing literary works by and about women and girls, conducted their own study of contemporary middle grade fiction of the late 1970s. They were looking to see if a heightened public awareness of racial and sex-role stereotypes had resulted in more diversity in the portrayal of females and males from a variety of racial and cultural groups. They found that the majority of juvenile novels still depicted white, middle-class families in fairly traditional gender roles.[33] However, they selected seventy-five titles with more diverse and positive portrayals, which were annotated, organized thematically, and published in the bibliography, *Books for Today's Young Readers.*[34]

In 1981 the authors of this book were hired to develop and coordinate the forerunner of Project Equal. It began as a one-year pilot program in eight New York City schools. Funded by the Rockefeller Family Fund and the New York Community Trust, the initial program was based on the premise that reading nonstereotyped juvenile fiction from the bibliography *Books for Today's Young Readers* would develop an awareness of stereotyping, change student perceptions of male and female roles, and improve student self-concept.

The project began with only a thematically annotated bibliography of children's books and the conviction that nonstereotyped juvenile literature could help children understand themselves and conceptualize a more equitable world. Some beginning criteria for book selection developed that summer as each of the seventy-five books was read and considered for inclusion in the program. In addition to issues of authenticity and literary quality, other questions emerged: Will students like this book and be able to relate to the characters? Does it hold the reader's attention? Is there a range of experiences and settings represented? (See Chapter 4 for a more extensive discussion of the process of formulating selection criteria for multicultural literature.)

The final list of twenty-five books chosen by project staff included a variety of settings and characters from diverse racial and cultural backgrounds on tour of the themes highlighted in the original bibliography: peer friendship, family relationships, the disabled young person, and intergenerational relationships. (As the program has evolved, books focusing on relationships with older people and children who are disabled have been incorporated into the friendship and family themes, and alternate themes of racial prejudice and discrimination and self awareness/identity have been introduced into the program. See Appendix for a list of Project Equal books organized by our current thematic groupings.) Geraldine Clark, Director of School Library Services for the New York City schools and a board member of The Feminist Press, helped to shape the original grant proposal and cosponsored the project. Four New York City districts were chosen to pilot the program based on the presence of active district library media coordinators and a student population representative of the cultural and racial diversity of New York City. The four coordinators identified two schools in each district (one elementary and one middle school) with competent, energetic library media specialists and principals likely to welcome a new program.

A Collaborative Staff-Development Model

A staff-development model was shaped that first year, with three all-day training sessions in the fall and weekly visits by the project facilitators from January through June. The collaborative model developed included team teaching and planning among the classroom teacher (elementary level) or the language arts teacher (middle school level), the school library media specialist, and the project facilitator. Recognizing that sex-role stereotyping might be a new and somewhat sensitive topic for many staff members, the three initial training sessions focused on issues of stereotyping, as well as samples of curriculum activities to be implemented in the classroom and library media center.

Each all-day training session covered a different area. The first session explored attitudes toward stereotyping, particularly gender stereotyping. The second session examined children's literature and stereotypes in books. The third session focused on the implementation of specific curriculum in awareness of stereotyping, literature, and women's history in the classroom and library. In each workshop participants were involved in hands-on consciousness-raising activities including interviews, role-plays, and values clarification, along with informational presentations and content analysis of books and audiovisual materials. (See Chapter 5 for specific examples of workshop activities.)

Weekly school visits by a project facilitator provided ongoing support for participating library media specialists and classroom teachers. Project facilitators modeled open-ended questioning, values clarification activities, and small group book discussions with the students. Frequent visits facilitated "bonding" between the project facilitators and the school staff, and regular planning sessions enabled the participants to discuss and reflect on the teaching process in a collegial atmosphere.

A Holistic Curriculum

Through working directly with the students on a weekly basis, a curriculum began to emerge. If students were to be able to recognize sex-role stereotypes in literature, they first had to understand the concept of stereotyping. Many young adolescents had never articulated their views of gender roles. Initial lessons, modeled by the project facilitator, helped students focus on the definition of stereotyping. A questionnaire was developed based on "Happy to Be Me," a film that surveyed the sex-role attitudes of New York City students.[35]

Although in 1981 when the program began many teachers and library media specialists had limited experience working together to integrate literature in a responsive, holistic language arts curriculum, frequent planning sessions with the project facilitator helped shift the focus to student concerns. Together the team discussed the students' responses during open-ended class discussions and reactions to books read independently. Teachers often shared insights about developmental issues that had arisen in the class and suggested such new areas for curriculum development as self-awareness activities. School library media specialists recommended novels that might be included in the program, possible research projects, and creative ways to report on books read independently.

Some of the initial awareness activities were adapted from curriculum guides on sex-role stereotyping. Other lessons such as surveys, writing activities, and role-playing scenarios were developed by the project staff to elicit student attitudes on gender roles, family relationships, and peer friendships. Each new lesson was field-tested as it was developed in the eight participating schools. The immediate feedback helped refine the lessons and indicated how students of different ages and abilities would respond to the curriculum.

Books were introduced according to the themes in the original bibliography, *Books for Today's Young Readers*. Discussion questions were written for each book to guide library media specialists and teachers as book discussion leaders. Small group book discussions in the library became an integral part of the program. Students shared their favorite books with the class through posters, dioramas, commercials, and dramatizations of scenes.

In 1983 the lessons developed during the first two years were formalized and published in the curriculum guide, *A Closer Look: An Interdisciplinary Approach to Stereotyping*.[36] This guide was updated in 1988, with additional lessons and discussion questions added on the themes of prejudice and discrimination and self-awareness. This "organic" approach to curriculum development continues to characterize the way that new lessons are created. For instance, when bilingual classes of new immigrants recently joined the program, a unit on immigration with a focus on realistic fiction and family histories describing the immigrant experience was developed and field-tested.

Institutionalizing the Program

How does an innovative pilot program become established as part of the ongoing curriculum in a school district? In 1983 grant funding ended and Project Equal had to establish an alternate source of support. A plan was worked out with the Central Board to sponsor Project Equal jointly through the Office of School Library Services and the participating school districts. Several factors in the following years became critical in the successful marketing and institutionalization of the program.

ADVOCACY

During the early years of the program, Geraldine Clark, Director of School Library Services for New York City, promoted and supported Project Equal as a model of library-classroom collaboration. Having a strong advocate at the Central Board proved critical for financial support in the transition from a grant-supported pilot effort to a self-sufficient program within the Office of School Library Services.

Those districts with active library media coordinators also supported the continuation of the program each year. Letters and phone calls from the library media specialists, teachers, and even students involved in the program helped convince the district supervisors that it was a worthwhile program that should continue.

ACCOUNTABILITY

Evaluation data was independently collected each year for several years, indicating that students had modified their perceptions of sex-role stereotypes and had increased independent reading. Evaluation reports were prepared each year and mailed to the participating superintendents and district liaisons.

RECRUITMENT

The project facilitators conducted district-wide training sessions each year for library media specialists, language arts teachers, and reading specialists to introduce the goals and methods of Project Equal. In addition, the project facilitators presented workshops on book selection, multicultural literature, and/or giving book talks at the annual city-wide conferences for school library media personnel. Participants often contacted their district supervisors after these workshops and requested to be involved in Project Equal.

PUBLICITY

A yearly newsletter with photographs, student work, and descriptions of the highlights of the program in each school was mailed to currently participating schools and schools that had completed the program.

A RESPONSIVE CURRICULUM

Although Project Equal began with a focus on sex-role stereotyping, the program evolved gradually over the years to develop a curriculum to sensitize students to other types of stereotyping (especially racial and ethnic stereotyping) and issues of prejudice and discrimination. This shift in focus was largely in response to the perceived needs of teachers and library media specialists for effective strategies to help students understand and appreciate the increasing racial and ethnic diversity in their schools and the larger community.

AN INTERDISCIPLINARY APPROACH

Recently a "whole language" approach to reading has gained popularity. Many schools have been looking for ways to transform their reading program to focus on children's literature as part of an integrated language arts curriculum. When the support shifted from a skills-based approach to a more holistic view of the reading process, Project Equal was one of the few established programs in New York City with a proven track record for infusing literature into the classroom. Many schools initially "bought into" the program as a literature program and only later realized the benefits students gained from a greater understanding of equity issues.

Why use multicultural literature to try to influence the way young adolescents see the world? What are the developmental issues that young people face, and why is a literature-based program uniquely suited to helping them explore those issues? The next two chapters will explore the program's rationale for the targeting of young adolescents for a multicultural literature program and for the use of realistic fiction to help them better understand themselves and others.

Notes

1. Theresa Inga, "What Is Project Equal?" *Project Equal Newsletter* 1 (Summer/Fall, 1990): 1.

2. Nicholas Zill, *U.S. Children and Their Families: Current Conditions and Recent Trends, 1989* (Washington, D.C.: Child Trends, 1989).

3. Children's Defense Fund, *The State of America's Children 1991* (Washington, D.C.: Children's Defense Fund, 1991).

4. Harold L. Hodgkinson, *All One System: Demographics of Education, Kindergarten through Graduate School* (Washington, D.C.: Institute for Educational Leadership, 1985), 3.

5. John O'Neil, "A Generation Adrift?" *Educational Leadership* 49 (Sept. 1991): 4–10.

6. Charlotte J. Patterson, "Children of Lesbian and Gay Parents," *Child Development* 63 (Oct. 1992): 1025–1042.

7. The Commission on Minority Participation in Education and American Life, *One-Third of a Nation* (Washington, D.C.: The American Council on Education, 1988).

8. Glen R. Elliott and S. Shirley Feldman, "Capturing the Adolescent Experience," in *At the Threshold: The Developing Adolescent,* ed. S. Shirley Feldman and Glen R. Elliott (Cambridge, Mass.: Harvard University Press, 1990), 1–13.

9. New York City Public Schools, "Pupil Ethnic Census," *Citywide Profile and Performance in Relation to Minimum Standards—1990–1991* (Brooklyn: New York City Public Schools), 6.

10. Doris R. Entwisle, "Schools and the Adolescent," in *At the Threshold: The Developing Adolescent,* ed. S. Shirley Feldman and Glen R. Elliott (Cambridge, Mass.: Harvard University Press, 1990), 197–224.

11. For a discussion of current issues in multicultural education see James A. Banks and Cherry A. McGee Banks, *Multicultural Education: Issues and Perspectives* (Needham Heights, Mass.: Allyn and Bacon, Inc., 1989); Christine E. Sleeter and Carl A. Grant, *Making Choices for Multicultural Education: Five Approaches to Race, Class, and Gender* (Columbus, Ohio: Merrill Pub. Co, 1988); Christine E. Sleeter, *Empowerment through Multicultural Education* (Albany, N.Y.: State University of New York Press, 1991).

12. For a critique of multicultural education see Dinesh D'Souza, *Illiberal Education: The Politics of Race and Sex on Campus* (New York: The Free Press, 1991); Arthur M. Schlesinger, Jr., *The Disuniting of America* (Knoxville, Tenn.: Whittle Direct Books, 1991); Diane Ravitch, "A Culture in Common," *Educational Leadership* 49 (Dec. 1991–Jan. 1992): 8–11.

13. Molefi Kete Asante, "Afrocentric Curriculum," *Educational Leadership* 49 (Dec.1991–Jan. 1992): 28–31.

14. Melinda Fine, "Facing History and Ourselves: Portrait of a Classroom," *Educational Leadership* 49 (Dec. 1991–Jan. 1992): 44–49.

15. Tom Roderick, "Johnny Can Learn to Negotiate," *Educational Leadership* 45 (Dec. 1987–Jan. 1988): 86–90.

16. Donna Norton, "Teaching Multicultural Literature in the Reading Curriculum," *Reading Teacher* 44 (Sept. 1990): 28–40; Timothy V. Rasinski and Nancy D. Padak, "Multicultural Learning through Children's Literature," *Language Arts* 67 (Oct. 1990): 576–580.

17. Jesse Perry, "Cultural Diversity through Literature," *The ALAN Review* 18 (Spring 1991): 45–47; Lyn Miller-Lachman, *Our Family, Our Friends, Our World: An Annotated Guide to Significant Multicultural Books for Children and Teenagers* (New York: Bowker, 1992).

18. James A. Banks, "Multicultural Education: Characteristics and Goals," in *Multicultural Education: Issues and Perspectives,* ed. James A. Banks and Cherry A. McGee Banks (Needham Heights, Mass.: Allyn and Bacon, Inc., 1989), 2–26.

19. New York City Board of Education, "Statement of Policy on Multicultural Education and Promotion of Positive Intergroup Relations," New York City Board of Education, 15 Nov. 1989.

20. Teri S. Lesesne, "Developing Lifetime Readers: Suggestions from Fifty Years of Research," *English Journal* 80 (Oct. 1991): 61–64.

21. O'Neil, "A Generation Adrift?" 8.

22. Margaret Meek, "What Counts as Evidence in Theories of Children's Literature?" *Theory into Practice* 21 (Autumn 1982): 284–292.

23. Kathryn P. Scott, "Effects of Gender–Fair Instructional Materials on Fourth, Seventh, and Eleventh Graders' Attitudes and Understanding," paper presented at the Annual Meeting of the American Educational Research Association, 1983.

24. Angelia Charleen Lindsey Josey, "A Comparison of Written Responses of Eleventh Grade Readers to Black and White Literature" (Ed.D. diss., Univ. of Georgia, 1990); Jean-Procope Martin, "The Effects of Selected Black Literature on the Attitudes of White Adolescents toward Blacks" (Ph.D. diss., Univ. of Connecticut, 1980); Jesse Perry, "Some Effects of Selected Black Literature on the Self Concept and Reading Achievement of Black Male Eighth Grade Students" (Ph.D. diss., Univ. of California-Berkeley, 1977).

25. Lee Galda, "Research in Response to Literature," *Journal of Research and Development in Education* 6 (Spring 1983): 1–6; Bernice E. Cullinan, Kathy T. Harwood, and Lee Galda, "The Reader and the Story: Comprehension and Response," *Journal of Research and Development in Education* 16 (Spring 1983): 29–38.

26. Belinda Y. Louie and Douglas H. Louie, "Empowerment through Young-Adult Literature," *English Journal* 81 (April 1992): 53–56.

27. Joanne M. Golden, "Reader-Text Interaction," *Theory into Practice* 25 (Spring 1986): 91–96; Susan M. Nugent, "Young Adult Literature: Opportunities for Thinking Critically," *The ALAN Review* 17 (Winter 1990): 4–7.

28. See the Bulletin and other publications from the Council for Interracial Books for Children, including *Guidelines for Selecting Bias-Free Textbooks and Storybooks* (New York: Council on Interracial Books for Children, 1980).

29. Nancy Larrick, "The All White World of Children's Books," *Saturday Review* 11 (11 April 1965): 63–65, 84–85.

30. Dorothy Broderick, *Image of the Black in Children's Fiction* (New York: Bowker, 1973).

31. Lenore Weitzman, Deborah Eifler, Elizabeth Hokada, and Catherine Ross, "Sex-Role Socialization in Picture Books for Preschool Children," *American Journal of Sociology* 77 (May 1972): 1125–1150.

32. Wilma H. Dougherty and Rosalind E. Engel, "An 80s Look for Sex Equality in Caldecott Winners and Honor Books," *The Reading Teacher* 40 (Jan. 1987): 394–398.

33. Jeanne Bracken and Sharon Wigutoff, "Sugar and Spice: That's What Children's Books Are Still Made of," *Emergency Librarian* 7 (Sept.–Dec. 1979): 1–3.

34. Jeanne Bracken and Sharon Wigutoff with Ilene Baker, *Books for Today's Young Readers* (Old Westbury, N.Y.: The Feminist Press, 1980).

35. Arthur Mokin, *Happy to Be Me* (Santa Rosa, Calif: Arthur Mokin Productions, Inc., 1979).

36. Lauri Johnson and Sally Smith, *A Closer Look: An Interdisciplinary Approach to Stereotyping* (Brooklyn: New York City Board of Education, 1988).

2

A Focus on Young Adolescents

Project Equal has brought out a side of me I never knew. Because of this project, I became aware of a value I never thought much about. This value is respect of self and others. I never thought of people respecting me because I'm just a kid, but now I know everyone deserves respect.

Claudio Martinez
Eighth Grade Student[1]

Adolescence is a distinct stage of life, a time of transition between childhood and adulthood with its own unique developmental issues. In the United States and most Western cultures, adolescence is generally viewed as extending from age ten or eleven through the late teens or early twenties, but the average length of adolescence may vary within racial, cultural, and/or socioeconomic groups.[2] Smith, in her review of the research on African American girls, reported that for poor black girls with increased family responsibilities, the end of adolescence may be age eighteen or even earlier.[3] On the other hand, adolescence may extend into the late twenties for upper middle-class college students pursuing graduate degrees who are financially supported by their parents. Social milestones such as becoming financially independent, joining the work force, or marrying have traditionally signaled the end of adolescence and the entry into adulthood.

The period of early adolescence (ages ten to fourteen) emerges as the time when students are making the transition from concrete thinking to more abstract reasoning, developing an awareness of multiple perspectives on an issue, and beginning to establish a unique identity. Young adolescents can evaluate the validity of information and distinguish fact from opinion. Since they can begin to grasp the abstract concept of stereotyping, they are a prime age group with which to implement a program that focuses on the acceptance of diversity.

Critical Developmental Issues of Early Adolescence

Jean Piaget and Erik Erikson, child development theorists who have historically had a significant impact on education, identify the cognitive and psychological changes associated with ten- to fourteen-year-old students. Piaget, focusing on the cognitive realm, refers to the period of late childhood (ages seven through eleven) as the time of concrete operations. Children can begin to sequence events, conceptualize, and make simple generalizations. According to Piaget, the stage of formal operations comes in early adolescence (ages eleven through fifteen). During this stage, students become more deductive in their reasoning, can link parts to the whole, and can assess the validity of information.[4]

In the psychological realm, Erikson characterizes early adolescence as a period of conflict between industry and inferiority. Middle graders look to the adult world for role models and feel inadequate if they can't show competence. In Erikson's view, later adolescence (ages twelve through twenty) is characterized by the conflict between identity and role diffusion in society. The adolescent begins to establish a separate identity by separating from the family.[5]

As our understanding of human development has evolved, new voices have entered the discussion, questioning how the psychological development of adolescents may be influenced by race, culture, and gender. Spencer and Dornbusch admit that research on children of color has often focused on a "deficit" model, examining negative outcomes rather than adaptive strategies. They caution researchers to examine cultural contexts and recognize the strengths and triumphs of children of color as well as the effects of prejudice and discrimination.[6]

Developmental issues that are central to all young adolescents in our diverse society include the roles of ethnicity and gender in the search for identity, attitudes toward other racial groups, the importance of peer relationships, and changing family configurations. Reading and discussing realistic fiction provides a nonthreatening way for young adolescents to explore their own developmental issues and develop acceptance of others.

Ethnic Identity Development

Achieving a sense of identity is one of the most important psychological tasks for the adolescent. This task requires the ability to know and understand oneself as an individual and to recognize one's place in society.[7] Early adolescents become aware of the choices they can make in terms of the extent to which they identify with their own racial and/or ethnic group. Theorists who have examined the development of ethnic identity point to early adolescence as a crucial time when children of color may experience an ethnic awakening, a conscious confrontation with this aspect of their personal and group identity.

Geneva Gay, building on a model developed by William Cross,[8] discusses how young adolescents become aware of the public image of their ethnic group and how their families and members of their group rank in the broader society in terms of success.[9] As their cognitive skills mature, adolescents more clearly see the relation of their group to the majority culture. In the words of Spencer and Dornbusch, "the young African American may learn as a child that black is beautiful but conclude as an adolescent that white is powerful."[10] Gay also points to new restrictions on interracial interactions during early adolescence. As physical maturity develops and puberty approaches, boys and girls from different racial groups who played together as nine-year-olds may find their parents discouraging cross-racial socializing at ages thirteen and fourteen.

In a more detailed discussion of the ethnic identity development process for African Americans, Gay describes the necessity for the individual to make a transformation from negative to positive identity, from an externally determined self-image to an internally self-defined "Black referent." She recommends using literature, such as novels written from an experiential, personal point of view, to help students learn useful strategies for resolving their own ethnic identity questions.[11]

One Project Equal book that directly addresses ethnic identity questions is *The Shimmershine Queens* (Yarbrough). Angie, the protagonist, is embarrassed to tell her mother that her sixth grade classmates tease her because of her dark skin and African facial features. Her visiting Great Cousin Seatta and the new African dance teacher at school help her gain pride in her African heritage. Through her work in the school play, Angie learns how to express that "shimmershine feeling" of confidence and self-respect.

Books with ethnic identity themes may relate more personally to children of

the particular racial or ethnic group depicted. Two African American girls who read *The Shimmershine Queens* termed it the "best book they had ever read" and asked if they could check the book out to read it again. Sims, in her article about how race and ethnicity may affect a reader's response to literature, found that her ten-year-old African American interviewee preferred to read books about "black girls like me."[12]

Ethnic identity issues also arise in the context of what it means to be an "American." After viewing the film entitled *A.M.E.R.I.C.A.N.S.,*[13] fifth grade Project Equal students who are recent immigrants described themselves as more Korean or more Russian than American because they spoke a different language at home and ate different food. Their definition of an "American" seems to be limited to someone who speaks only English and eats "typically" American food like hamburgers and hot dogs. Immigrant students who have been in the United States for a longer period of time report identifying with this simplified vision of "American" culture at school and with their family's culture at home, especially if their families continue to speak their native languages and practice religious and cultural traditions at home that differ from those of their classmates.

Children in multiethnic classrooms often don't discuss cultural and religious differences for fear that other students might tease them or misinterpret their traditions. During a class discussion on prejudice in a racially and culturally diverse class of recent immigrants, two Pakistani boys revealed that they had surreptitiously sat in the school lunchroom for a month without eating because they were observing the Moslem holiday Ramadan and were required to fast from sunrise to sunset. They hadn't told the teacher or their classmates because they felt no one would understand.

Books depicting the immigrant experience can help young adolescents struggle with issues of cultural identity and assimilation. Shirley, in *In the Year of the Boar and Jackie Robinson* (Lord), emigrates in 1947 from an extended family household in China to a small apartment in Brooklyn, shared with her mother and father. The only Chinese girl in her class, Shirley struggles to learn English on her own and feels confused by much of the school routine. Through a friendship with another classmate she develops an interest in baseball and begins to feel more accepted in the class. She still speaks Chinese with her parents, but, finding herself substituting English expressions, she begins to wonder, "Now that she was thinking more and more in English . . . was her black hair turning blond? Was her nose getting higher? If she had a choice she'd just as soon stay the same."

Reading about Shirley's efforts to become bicultural, to be an American without giving up her Chinese identity, can help other immigrant students explore their own ethnic identity questions. A Chinese American boy who read the book said he felt lonely like Shirley when he first came to this country and couldn't speak English. An eighth grade student discussing *Harriet's Daughter* (Philip), another Project Equal book about the immigrant experience, said she identified with Zulma, a girl who has just moved to Toronto from the Caribbean and is teased because of her accent and dress. "That's me all over!" the student said.

The Influence of Gender

Traditional models of psychological development have also failed to take into consideration the impact of gender during adolescence. Gilligan, in a ground-breaking and still controversial study of moral development in adult women, revealed that Kohlberg's original research on the stages of moral development had been based on exclusively male samples. She outlined an alternative theory of adult female moral development that focused more on caring, connectedness, and responsibility for others.[14]

When Gilligan and her colleagues at the Harvard Center for the Development and Study of Gender, Education, and Human Development began to focus on adolescent girls, they found a similar lack of female samples. In the words of a major textbook on adolescent psychology, "girls have simply not been much studied."[15]

The work of the Harvard Center and other researchers has begun to focus attention on the adolescent female experience. In a longitudinal study of young adolescents in a private girls' school, Brown and Gilligan found that girls who were confident at eleven became unsure of their knowledge and insecure at age sixteen.[16] Brown targets fifth grade as a critical time for girls, when ten- and eleven-year-olds are still confident to speak about what they feel and think.

Responses to Project Equal surveys collected over several years corroborate this finding. Fifth and sixth grade girls have written positively about themselves, mentioning that they liked being a girl because girls have better friendships, and expressing the belief that they were intelligent and could do more things than boys could do. Brown recommends that teachers, particularly women teachers, establish connections with girls before they begin to withdraw, "lose their voice," and become silent about their knowledge of relationships.[17] Gilligan has described adolescence as "a crisis of connection for girls coming of age in Western culture," in which they feel they must choose between being good (abandoning the self) or being selfish in pursuing their own goals.[18] Gilligan's critics caution against basing a developmental model on such a small exclusive sample and express concern about dichotomizing boys' and girls' experiences in ways that may reinforce gender stereotypes.[19]

THE EFFECT OF GENDER STEREOTYPES ON DEVELOPMENT

Researchers have found that girls may experience some developmental issues during adolescence differently from boys. A recent national survey by the American Association of University Women found that self-esteem drops significantly during early adolescence for many girls, possibly influenced by their school experiences.[20] Simmons reports that the move from elementary school to junior high appears to be particularly difficult for girls. The transition to a large, impersonal school with several different teachers and the changing of classes can be disorienting.[21] Adolescent girls are also more likely than boys to have a negative body image and rely more on the evaluations of others as their measure of self-worth.[22]

Increased family responsibilities during adolescence can signal additional sources of stress for girls. Colton and Gore found that girls are significantly more vulnerable than boys to practical involvement in their mothers' problems and emotional involvement in family difficulties.[23] A review of the research on female dropouts notes that young women are most at risk for dropping out when they live in low income households with multiple siblings.[24] These are the girls who are expected, during adolescence, to take on such adult responsibilities as cooking dinner, cleaning the house, and taking care of younger brothers and sisters.

Teenage pregnancy is still a growing national problem. For adolescent girls, becoming pregnant often means the end of formal education.[25] Even with an equivalent education, women will still earn less than men (70 cents for every dollar)[26] and will often have to support their children by themselves.

For adolescent boys, pressures to be competitive and suppress their emotions can also pay a toll in the structured school environment. Boys who have been socialized to be active and aggressive encounter conflicting expectations at school, resulting in a disproportionate number of boys cited as discipline problems, grade repeaters, and in need of remedial programs.[27] Boys who do not fit the traditional male stereotype of high achievement in academics or excellence in competitive sports may feel a sense of failure and "disconnect" from school.

THE IMPACT OF RACE AND ETHNICITY ON GIRLS

There appear to be important interactions between race and girls' self-esteem. Black girls in elementary schools express high levels of self-esteem that they retain through high school. While positive family and community support helps sustain a general sense of self-worth, African American girls feel strong pressure from the school system and drop significantly in positive feelings about their teachers and their school work during adolescence. Poor black girls, in particular, find they must "shut off" an unresponsive educational system in order to sustain a positive sense of who they are.[28]

Hispanic girls in a study by the American Association of University Women showed the greatest drop in self-esteem from elementary to high school. They were insecure about appearance, family relationships, school, talents, and their own importance.[29] According to a study by Fine and Zane, low income urban Latinas are most at risk for dropping out of school.[30] Zane, in a separate study of female dropouts, also found that low income African American and low income Hispanic girls often perceived school as irrelevant to their needs.[31]

Asian American girls' development has not been widely studied, perhaps because of the cultural stereotype that they are a "model minority" with few problems. Nagata suggests that the stress associated with living up to the "achieving Asian" stereotype, along with parental pressures for school achievement, may result in negative developmental experiences for some individuals.[32]

STUDENT ATTITUDES TOWARD GENDER ROLES

Student views of appropriate behavior and roles for females and males vary based on sex, age, cultural background, and range of experiences. In Project Equal we have found that fifth and sixth graders as a group are more accepting of a variety of behaviors for boys and girls, but they are also more grounded in their concrete reality. In an introductory activity in the program, students are asked to state their views of gender roles in a survey format. When asked to name the difference between boys and girls, two fifth grade boys had difficulty understanding that "long hair" and "skirts" might not be valid differences, especially if other cultures and historical periods were considered. Their experiences in the school and the immediate neighborhood formed the basis for the only valid distinctions in their minds.

A female student in the same class looked at the list on the board, which included "long hair/short hair, two earrings/one earring, different toys, weak/strong, more body hair, girls wear makeup, skirts/pants" and commented, "But none of those things are important," and mentioned "different body parts" as the difference. By seventh and eighth grade, students can focus on salient sex differences, but they may not be willing to discuss the topic as openly as fifth graders.

Other questions on the survey of sex roles highlight the differences in the way that boys and girls view gender roles. The question, "Is it all right for a man to cry?" has elicited the response, "Why is this question on here?" from a sophisticated seventh grade boy, "No! Because men own the world" from a fifth grade boy, and, probably the most common response from girls, "Yes, men have feelings, too."

Just as literature can help children explore ethnic identity questions, realistic fiction can also help students focus on changing definitions of gender roles. A Project Equal book that addresses gender stereotyping is *The Real Me* (Miles). The protagonist, Barbara Fisher, is angry when she realizes she can't be on the tennis team at her school because girls are not allowed to enroll in the tennis class and must take slimnastics instead. She begins a successful petition drive to include girls on the tennis team. Three sixth grade girls who read this book proudly informed their teacher that they had initiated a petition for girls to join the basketball team in their school. With their teacher's assistance, they presented their principal with the signed petition. "We told him we got the idea from *The Real Me*," they said.

Other books more subtly help girls and boys think about the range of gender roles. Charlie in *Charlie Pippin* (Walter) and Maudie and Kate in *Maudie and Me and the Dirty Book* (Miles) are girls who take the initiative and stand up for what they believe. Leigh Botts in *Dear Mr. Henshaw* (Cleary) explores his feelings about his parents' divorce and his loneliness in a series of letters and diary entries.

Attitudes toward Other Racial Groups

Most studies that have examined children's attitudes toward other racial groups have focused on preschool children, using dolls or photographs to elicit children's responses. By age three, young children can identify skin color and other racial cues.[33] During the preschool and early elementary years prevailing social attitudes and realities become associated with observed physical differences. Katz points to the importance of school experiences (or lack of them) with children and adults of other races and suggests that the attitudes of teachers and peers can be a critical influence on children's developing attitudes.[34]

Some researchers have reported a drop in prejudicial attitudes at age eight.[35] By the late elementary years, however, children's ideas and feelings related to racial differences have crystallized. The concepts of "us" versus "them" and intergroup differences become accentuated.[36]

There is a surprising lack of studies about the racial attitudes of young adolescents. Two ethnographic studies, one of an interracial middle school and the other at the high school level, found that peers discouraged intergroup contact and that students' perceptions of other racial groups had hardened.[37] Formal measures of young adolescents' attitudes toward other racial groups become difficult because students are aware of the desirable responses. By age ten or eleven they realize that expressing negative attitudes toward other racial and ethnic groups may not be supported by the teacher or examiner.[38]

The young adolescent is developmentally ready, however, to discuss the general concept of stereotyping and begin to understand how limited perceptions can affect one's behavior toward others. An awareness activity in Project Equal, "Definitions/Unfinished Sentences," requires students to use their experiences and knowledge to define a stereotype and generate examples of common stereotypes they have heard or encountered. It is stressed that the stereotypes they use as examples do not represent their own feelings or opinions. The teacher or library media specialist presenting the lesson can begin with such examples as, "All Koreans own vegetable stores" or "All women are weak" or point out the preponderance of television commercials portraying Italian Americans eating or preparing pasta. The fallacies in these overgeneralized statements and observations are pointed out in a nonthreatening atmosphere.

Students also generate a list of groups that are stereotyped in our society. They may suggest homeless people, people with AIDS, teenagers, African Americans, Hispanics/Latinos, gays/lesbians, people with disabilities, etc. Most classes are able, when focused explicitly on the topic, to recognize a large number of groups who experience prejudice.

SOURCES OF PREJUDICE

Allport defines prejudice as an overcategorization in which children assume that people in the same category will behave, look, feel, and think the same.[39] Although there are no clear causes of prejudice, there are numerous theories and explanations. Katz points out that although common sense would suggest that children learn prejudice from their parents, research has not shown a consistent correlation between parents' expressed attitudes and children's attitudes,[40] possibly because of the difficulty of accurately assessing parents' points of view. On the other hand, Ramsey suggests that parents' implicit actions, such as expressing fear in certain neighborhoods and associating only with members of their own racial group, may convey subtle messages of prejudice to their children.[41] In Project Equal we have found that young adolescents are very aware of their parents' prejudicial attitudes. Some students will acknowledge that their parents don't want them to associate with someone of a different race, and that they don't invite certain friends to their homes for this reason.

Aboud, in her review of research on prejudice, outlines three basic theories on the sources of prejudice: social reflection, inner state, and social-cognitive.[42] The social reflection theory argues that prejudice reflects the differential status given to different ethnic groups in a stratified society. Children adopt attitudes corresponding to the social structure as perceived by their parents and significant others. This theory recognizes that some groups have more power and privilege than others, and that children are more likely to express prejudice toward groups of lower status. Ramsey cites a study that found that young white children consistently associated shabby clothes and poor housing with black dolls rather than with white dolls.[43] Without an understanding of the negative effects of discrimination, young children assume that the individual is to blame for his or her poverty. Aboud acknowledges that the social reflection theory helps explain which groups in our society will experience the most prejudice, but it doesn't account for why some individuals are more prejudiced than others and why children's attitudes take different forms at different developmental stages.

The inner state theory explains prejudice in terms of an unresolved internal conflict. In this theory, prejudiced people tend to have parents who imposed rigid conventional rules of conduct on them as children. They can't express their hostility to their parents, so they displace this hostility onto people who lack authority and power. Like the social reflection theory, this theory fails to account for developmental stages of prejudice.

Dissatisfaction with the developmental aspects of these two classical theories of prejudice led to the emergence of social-cognitive developmental theories of prejudice. These theories predict different types of prejudices at different ages as a result of changes in cognitive structure. Based on Piaget's developmental stages, young children (ages three through eight) at the stage of preoperational thought focus on visually salient features and tend to overgeneralize, applying evaluative statements to everyone in a particular group. Egocentric in their interpretation of events and information, they are limited in their ability to see information objectively or from multiple points of view.

When children enter the concrete operations stage (ages eight through eleven), they move beyond one-dimensional thinking and make simple generalizations. Some researchers have found a drop in prejudicial attitudes between ages eight and ten. As mentioned earlier, students appear to become more rigid in their attitudes as they enter adolescence.

Social stratification, displaced hostility, cognitive development, and other aspects of each of these theories may explain the development of prejudice in particular individuals. Certainly children are influenced by changing societal views of particular racial and ethnic groups. Ramsey and Katz found that young African American children are more likely to identify positive connotations with being black since the advent of the civil rights and Black Power movements of the 1960s.

Classmates, older siblings, and friends can also have a significant influence on prejudicial attitudes. Ethnic jokes become a popular means of cementing in-group relationships for preadolescents. In a panel discussion on racial attitudes in New York City, a multiracial group of thirteen- and fourteen-year-olds confirmed that they wouldn't openly challenge a friend who was telling an ethnic joke or making racist comments.

It is clear that more research needs to be conducted on children's racial attitudes, particularly with older children and young adolescents. Surveys and class discussions in Project Equal indicate that students are sometimes reluctant to discuss their attitudes, especially in racially mixed classes. Children who have personally experienced prejudice may be more sensitive and aware of the issues. Phinney and Tarver, in a study of ethnic identity development among black and white eighth graders, found that the African American students had a better understanding of prejudice and knowledge of their own culture than did the white students.[44]

Peer Relationships

Finding friends that are accepting and supportive and can share their interests is one of the most important psychological tasks for young adolescents. As they begin to move away from their families to establish their own identity, young people substitute their friends as a source of psychological dependence.[45] Young adolescents often feel that they can be more open with their friends than with their families and can reveal their true selves. In describing what's important in a friendship, adolescents focus on different qualities than do young children. Most important, friends must be loyal, and "not talk about you behind your back." Creating intimacy and being able to share one's thoughts and feelings honestly is also important.[46]

Do boys and girls have different types of friendships? Some researchers have found that boys' friendship needs are met through actions and deeds and girls' needs through the disclosure of personal thoughts and feelings. Girls often perceive their friendships as more intimate and emotionally supportive than do boys.[47] Project Equal surveys and discussions on friendship seem to confirm these differences. Girls and boys often list differing activities that they engage in with their friends. Boys say they play sports, video games, or go to the movies together. Girls are more likely to talk on the phone, go shopping, visit each other's homes, and share secrets.

Is it difficult to be close friends with someone of the opposite sex? When asked to indicate their closest friends, most young adolescents tended to select same-sex, same-race best friends. Friendships between boys and girls have not been extensively studied. Savin-Williams and Berndt point out that these friendships may play a special role in the development of empathy and altruism and should be examined more closely.[48]

During values clarification activities and class discussions with Project Equal classes, fifth and sixth grade students theoretically agree that boys and girls can be close friends. When asked if it happens in real life, most students say that they have friends of the opposite sex but admit that their best friends are of the same sex. Older seventh and eighth grade students are more aware of the problems associated with opposite-sex friendships. They mention that boys and girls may have different interests and that other people may assume it's a romantic relationship.

Characters in books can serve as referents to help young adolescents expand and refine their concept of friendship. Two books used in Project Equal, *The Gift Giver* (Hansen) and *Bridge to Terabithia* (Paterson), show friendships between boys and girls, friendships based on respect and shared interest, which persist despite teasing from family or peers. Amir and Doris in *The Gift Giver* and Leslie and Jesse in *Bridge to Terabithia* create private worlds of friendship that enable them to grow and gain in self-confidence and understanding. During a "Values Line-Up" activity with a group of sixth graders, one girl strongly disagreed with the statement, "It's impossible for boys and girls to be friends." "Look at Doris and Amir. They're close friends in *The Gift Giver*," was her reply.

Behaving to avoid disapproval of peers may diminish with age. The importance of belonging to a crowd peaks in early adolescence and then decreases as older teenagers become more dissatisfied with the conformity that a group demands. Parents and teachers worry about the negative influences of peer groups, but research shows that young adolescents are more likely to follow their parents' advice in matters concerning their long-term future, such as college choices or career planning.[49] Friends' influence is magnified when adolescents perceive that their relationship with parents is negative or lacking in support.[50]

Rubin reminds us that through friendship children learn such social skills as the ability to empathize and understand the point of view of others. However, they also learn how to reject others, stereotype them, and engage in antisocial behavior.[51] Juvenile fiction can highlight these negative influences in instructive ways. For example, twelve-year-old Jamal in the book *Scorpions* (Myers) experiences pressure to take over his older brother's gang. Although he clearly sees the problems and dangers of gang life, he is also searching for male role models, and the power and visibility of the gang members and their weapons are appealing. Three other Project Equal novels, *Daphne's Book* (Hahn), *Maudie and Me and the Dirty Book* (Miles), and *Between Friends* (Garrigue) focus on the pressure felt by young adolescent girls to ostracize and not pursue friendships with unpopular classmates or neighbors. Daphne is the class outcast, a shabbily dressed child from a troubled family. Maudie is not part of the in-crowd in her new middle school and is a little overweight, while Dede, the would-be friend in *Between Friends,* is a young adolescent with Down syndrome.

Family Relationships

Despite the growing influence of peers, the family continues to exert the most powerful impact on young adolescents. Parental influence is greatest during the years of early childhood and is then ideally transformed during early adolescence to reflect an interdependence in which close ties are maintained without threat to the young adolescent's individuality. In contrast to the popular conception of adolescence as a time of storm and stress, Steinberg reports that 75 percent of families surveyed have experienced warm and pleasant relationships during the adolescent years.[52]

There are new challenges for today's youth, however. Over the last twenty-five years, the American family has emerged in a variety of configurationsd. The divorce rate is 50 percent; many students experience their parents' divorce and are required to adjust to life in a single parent family or a "blended" family if one or both of their parents remarry. With the majority of mothers with school-age children in the work force, many young adolescents, especially girls, come home each day to increased household responsibilities, often including care of a younger brother or sister. Children may feel resentful that they have less free time. Some students may feel ambivalent about their parents' divorce, recognizing that there is less conflict in the family, but still holding out hope that their parents will get back together.

Project Equal books on the family theme depict the ten- to fourteen-year-old protagonist beginning to see his or her family in a more objective way, with a greater understanding of others' perspectives. In *Dear Mr. Henshaw* (Cleary), Leigh comes grudgingly to accept the fact that however much he wishes it, he cannot will his divorced parents back together. His parents have separate lives and needs and he must learn to make a place for himself in both their lives. Older readers find Neil, the protagonist of *Welcome Home Jellybean* (Shyer), facing an increasingly complex home life when his retarded older sister comes to live with him and his parents. Eventually he must choose between separating himself from his sister and her problems or remaining as a strong family link. Dicey, beginning a new life with her grandmother in *Dicey's Song* (Voigt), finds her younger siblings don't depend completely on her anymore, and she must make the transition to becoming a "normal" teenager with a life of her own.

Young adolescents are uniquely suited to an intervention program designed to promote acceptance of diversity. Their greater cognitive maturity enables them to look at situations from a variety of viewpoints, to recognize the difference between fact and opinion, and to critically examine the validity of information. By ten and eleven years of age, children are capable of looking beyond their concrete reality to recognize that other families and communities may be different from their own. Their sense of justice and fairness in their own lives is keen, and they can begin to empathize with others who have been treated unfairly. Chapter 3 will outline the philosophical assumptions underlying the use of multicultural literature to develop these capabilities and will discuss student responses to developmental themes and issues raised in the books.

Notes

1. Claudio Martinez, "What Project Equal Means to Me," *Project Equal Newsletter* 1 (Summer/Fall, 1990), 8.

2. Glen R. Elliott and S. Shirley Feldman, "Capturing the Adolescent Experience," in *At the Threshold: The Developing Adolescent,* ed. S. Shirley Feldman and Glen R. Elliott (Cambridge, Mass.: Harvard University Press, 1990), 1–13.

3. Elsie Smith, "The Black Female Adolescent: A Review of the Educational, Career, and Psychological Literature," *Psychology of Women Quarterly* 6 (Spring 1982): 261–288.

4. Dorothy G. Singer and Tracey A. Revenson, *A Piaget Primer: How a Child Thinks* (New York: New American Library, 1978).

5. Erik H. Erikson, *Childhood and Society,* 35th anniv. ed. (New York: W. W. Norton, 1986).

6. Margaret Beale Spencer and Sanford M. Dornbusch with the assistance of Randy Mont-Reynaud, "Challenges in Studying Minority Youth," in *At the Threshold: The Developing Adolescent,* ed. S. Shirley Feldman and Glen R. Elliott (Cambridge, Mass.: Harvard University Press, 1990), 123–146.

7. Doreen Rosenthal, "Ethnic Identity Development in Adolescents," in *Children's Ethnic Socialization: Pluralism and Development,* ed. Jean S. Phinney and Mary Jane Rotheram (Newbury Park, Calif.: Sage Publications, 1987), 156–179.

8. William E. Cross, Jr., "A Two Factor Theory of Black Identity: Implications for the Study of Identity Development in Minority Children," in *Children's Ethnic Socialization: Pluralism and Development,* ed. Jean S. Phinney and Mary J. Rotheram (Newbury Park, Calif.: Sage Publications, 1987), 117–133.

9. Geneva Gay, "Ethnic Identity in Early Adolescence: Some Implications for Instructional Reform," *Educational Leadership* 35 (May 1978): 649–655.

10. Spencer and Dornbusch, "Challenges in Studying Minority Youth," 129.

11. Geneva Gay, "Implications of Selected Models of Ethnic Identity Development for Educators," *Journal of Negro Education* 54 (Winter 1985): 43–55.

12. Rudine Sims, "Strong Black Girls: A Ten Year Old Responds to Fiction about Afro-Americans," *Journal of Research and Development in Education* 16 (Spring 1983): 21–28.

13. Steven Okazaki, *A.M.E.R.I.C.A.N.S.* (Los Angeles: Churchill Films, 1980).

14. Carol Gilligan, *In a Different Voice: Psychological Theory and Women's Development* (Cambridge, Mass.: Harvard University Press, 1982).

15. Joseph Adelson and Margery Doehrman, "The Psychodynamic Approach to Adolescence," in *Handbook of Adolescent Psychology,* ed. Joseph Adelson (New York: John Wiley, 1980), 114.

16. Lyn M. Brown and Carol Gilligan, *The Psychology of Women and the Development of Girls* (Cambridge, Mass.: Harvard University Center for the Study of Gender, Education, and Human Development, 1990).

17. Lyn M. Brown, *A Problem of Vision: The Development of Relational Voice in Girls Ages 7 to 16* (Cambridge, Mass.: Harvard Center for the Development and Study of Gender, Education, and Human Development, 1990).

18. Carol Gilligan, "Teaching Shakespeare's Sister: Notes from the Underground of Female Adolescence," in *Making Connections: The Relational Worlds of Adolescent Girls at Emma Willard School,* ed. Carol Gilligan, Nona Lyons, and Trudy J. Hanmer (Cambridge, Mass.: Harvard University Press, 1990), 9.

19. Anne Colby and William Damon, "Listening to a Different Voice: A Review of Gilligan's *In a Different Voice,*" *Merrill-Palmer Quarterly* 29 (Oct. 1983): 473–481.

20. American Association of University Women, *Shortchanging Girls, Shortchanging America* (Washington, D.C.: AAUW, 1991), 11.

21. Roberta Simmons and D. Blythe, *Moving into Adolescence* (Hawthorne, N.Y.: Aldine de Gruyter, 1987).

22. Susan Harter, "Self and Identity Development," in *At the Threshold: The Developing Adolescent,* ed. S. Shirley Feldman and Glen R. Elliott (Cambridge, Mass.: Harvard University Press, 1990), 352–387.

23. Mary Ellen Colton and Susan Gore, *Adolescent Stress: Causes and Consequences* (Hawthorne, N.Y.: Aldine de Gruyter, 1991).

24. Janice Earle, Virginia Roach, with Katherine Fraser, *Female Dropouts: A New Perspective* (Alexandria, Va: National Association of State Boards of Education, 1987).

25. American Association of University Women, *The AAUW Report: How Schools Shortchange Girls* (Washington, D.C.: 1992), 39.

26. Ibid., 4.

27. Myra Sadker and David Sadker, *The Report Card: The Cost of Sex Bias in Schools* (Washington, D.C.: Mid-Atlantic Center for Sex Equity, The American University, 1981).

28. American Association of University Women, *Shortchanging Girls, Shortchanging America,* 8.

29. *Shortchanging Girls,* 9.

30. Michelle Fine and Nancie Zane, "Being Wrapped Too Tight: When Low Income Women Drop out of High School," in *Dropouts from School,* ed. Lois Weis and Hugh G. Petrie (Albany, N.Y.: SUNY Press, 1989), 23–53.

31. Nancie Zane, *In Our Own Voices* (Washington, D.C.: Project on Equal Education Rights, 1988).

32. Donna Nagata, "Japanese American Children and Adolescents," in *Children of Color,* ed. Jewelle T. Gibbs and Larke N. Huang (San Francisco: Jossey-Bass, 1991), 67–113.

33. Phyllis A. Katz, "Development of Children's Racial Awareness of Intergroup Attitudes," in *Current Topics in Early Childhood Education,* Vol. 4, ed. L. G. Katz (Norwood, N.J.: Ablex Publishing Corp., 1982), 17–54.

34. Ibid., 48.

35. Frances Aboud, *Children and Prejudice* (New York: Blackwell, Inc., 1988), 30.

36. Katz, "Development of Children's Racial Awareness of Intergroup Attitudes," 47.

37. Janet Ward Schofield, "Complementary and Conflicting Identities: Images and Interactions in an Interracial School," in *The Development of Children's Friendships,* ed. Steven R. Asher and John M. Gottman (New York: Cambridge University Press, 1981), 53–90; Martin Patchen, *Black-White Contact in Schools: Its Social and Academic Effects* (West Lafayette, Ind.: Purdue University Press, 1982).

38. Patricia Ramsey, *Teaching and Learning in a Diverse World: Multicultural Education for Young Children* (New York: Teachers College Press, 1987).

39. Gordon W. Allport, *The Nature of Prejudice* (New York: Doubleday, 1958).

40. Katz, "Development of Children's Racial Awareness of Intergroup Attitudes," 26.

41. Ramsey, *Teaching and Learning in a Diverse World,* 36.

42. Aboud, *Children and Prejudice,* 17–27.

43. Ramsey, *Teaching and Learning in a Diverse World,* 34.

44. Jean S. Phinney and Steve Tarver, "Ethnic Identity Search and Commitment in Black and White Eighth Graders," *Journal of Early Adolescence* 8 (Fall 1988): 265–277.

45. B. Bradford Brown, "Peer Groups and Peer Cultures," in *At the Threshold: The Developing Adolescent,* ed. S. Shirley Feldman and Glen R. Elliott (Cambridge, Mass.: Harvard University Press, 1990), 171–196.

46. Ritch C. Savin-Williams and Thomas J. Berndt, "Friendship and Peer Relations," in *At the Threshold: The Developing Adolescent,* ed. S. Shirley Feldman and Glen R. Elliott (Cambridge, Mass.: Harvard University Press, 1990), 277–307.

47. Ibid., 289.

48. Ibid., 304.

49. Hans Sebald and Becky White, "Teenagers' Divided Reference Groups: Uneven Alignment with Parents and Peers," *Adolescence* 15 (Winter 1980): 979–984.

50. Brown, "Peer Groups and Peer Cultures," 174.

51. Zick Rubin, *Children's Friendships* (Cambridge, Mass.: Harvard University Press, 1980).

52. Laurence Steinberg, "Autonomy, Conflict, and Harmony in the Family Relationship," in *At the Threshold: The Developing Adolescent,* ed. S. Shirley Feldman and Glen R. Elliott (Cambridge, Mass.: Harvard University Press, 1990), 255–276.

3

The Rationale for a Literature-Based Program

Reading is the sole means by which we slip, involuntarily, often helplessly, into another's skin, another's voice, another's soul.

> Joyce Carol Oates
> *The Reader's Quotation Book:*
> *A Literary Companion* [1]

As teachers and librarians we have often seen the effect that a particular book can have on a child's life. Project Equal began with the philosophical assumption that children's literature can, in the words of Charlotte Huck, "educate the heart as well as the mind."[2] Through reading and identifying with the characters in a book, children can enhance their self-concept, gain insight into their own culture, and develop empathy with people from other communities and different life experiences.

Creating a Community of Interactive Readers

The teaching strategies used in Project Equal classrooms grow from the following fundamental assumptions about reading and literature.

1. *Reading is an interactional process between the story and the reader.* Based on the work of Louise Rosenblatt, this approach views the act of reading as a two-way process, with reader and text forming a kind of "live circuit." From this view, reading is not a search for the "one right meaning." Instead, meaning is shaped by the ideas, beliefs, and values that each student brings to the books he or she reads.[3] When students read realistic novels that emphasize diversity, they encounter an author's perspective of the world that may be different from their own. In small group discussions, the teacher and library media specialist become literary guides to help students appreciate the author's perspective and also elicit the students' responses to what they have read.

31

2. *Reading is a social act.* Hepler and Hickman, reporting on ethnographic studies of the use of literature in elementary school classrooms, found that the selection of books and responses to those books were very much influenced by social interactions. Friends often recommended books to each other and shared their reactions together. The teacher became a reading role model, providing access and recommending books, and showing enjoyment in reading to her students. According to Hepler and Hickman, the effective classroom reading program creates a "community of readers" who communicate together about books.[4]

In Project Equal, the classroom teacher, library media specialist, and project facilitator create a "community of readers" in a particular classroom by establishing an atmosphere where everyone has a "reason to read" and by providing ways for both students and staff to share their responses to books with each other. Some schools have a silent reading period each day when everyone reads, including the teacher. In other classrooms the teacher may read an entire novel aloud to the students in daily installments.

Independent reading is motivated through book talks about Project Equal books on a theme such as families or peer pressure. Teachers and library media specialists also share their personal responses to books, letting students know when they disagree. Students are encouraged to share their reactions to books they have read independently by recommending books or reading aloud journal entries to the class.

Reading can even be a communal act outside the classroom or library media center. In one school two seventh grade boys mentioned they like to check out the same book so they can read to each other on the school bus. In a different school, a teacher reported that her students took the Project Equal novels to the lunchroom each day so that they could read together after they finished eating. A literate environment is created when students and staff share books together.

3. *Different readers respond differently to the same book.* A review of research on reader response to literature found that children's responses can be affected by age, ability level, gender, and the type of text read.[5] Sims also suggests that racial and cultural background may affect how students respond to literature.[6] In Project Equal, fifth through eighth grade students from diverse racial and cultural backgrounds and ability levels may read the same book and express a variety of responses. Some books, such as *The Pinballs* (Byars), a story about three children with problems who come together in a foster home, seem to be universally liked and understood by both boys and girls of different ages. The ability of the characters to move beyond adversity and learn to be "family" for each other seems to resonate for older children and young adolescents alike.

Other books, such as *Scorpions* (Myers), evoke different responses from older boys than from girls or younger students. Often a book discussion group on *Scorpions* will contain only boys, because girls are less likely to choose this book to read independently. Seventh and eighth grade boys characterize it as the "best book they ever read" and have a more personal response, talking about pressures they feel to "act tough" and not show fear or uncertainty that could be interpreted as a sign of weakness. Some boys identify with Jamal, the quiet artist who is attracted to the gang, thinking that he may gain more respect from his older brother and Dwayne, the class bully, if he joins the Scorpions. Others identify with Tito, Jamal's best friend, who tries to persuade him not to get involved with the gang, but stands by Jamal in the end, with tragic consequences.

On the other hand, some fifth and sixth graders who have read *Scorpions* report that it was "boring" or "too depressing." One sixth grade girl identified with Sassy, Jamal's younger sister, a "good girl" who threatens to tell her mother about Jamal's involvement with the gang. Perhaps older girls are less attracted to this book because this male coming-of-age story relates less directly to their developmental needs.

In small group discussions, students often relate personal experiences that they have had that are similar to those of the characters in the books. Foreman-Peck found that this "personalizing" of the story helped other group members understand each other's perspectives.[7] In a book discussion on *Welcome Home Jellybean* (Shyer), a fifth grade boy commented that he felt this story about a severely retarded girl's homecoming after years in an institution must have been written "just for him." This student revealed that he had a retarded brother and had experienced some of the same ambivalent feelings Geraldine's brother Neil experiences in the book. Other students in the group had a better understanding of the challenges of family life with a sibling who is developmentally disabled after this discussion.

4. *Discussion of literature can create a deeper understanding of what is read.* Through group discussion of a novel they have read independently, students voice their own interpretations and gain insight from other students' responses to the same text. Golden found that eighth graders discovered what they thought about a story through talk.[8] Group discussion became central to helping students clarify aspects of the story and construct a shared meaning.

Eeds and Wells, in a naturalistic study of literature discussion groups of fifth and sixth grade students, reported that the students could engage in real "dialogue" about a novel they read when the teacher moved beyond an inquisitional style and encouraged students to share their personal responses to the story.[9] Talking helped to confirm, extend, and modify the students' individual interpretations of the book.

In Project Equal, novels read are discussed in small groups as an integral and ongoing part of the program. The classroom teacher, library media specialist, and project facilitator each lead groups simultaneously in

the library. For children who may be confused about certain aspects of a particular book, the meaning is often clarified in these discussions. Some-times literal facts about characters or situations in the novels are discussed. How did Harvey end up with two broken legs in *The Pinballs* (Byars)? What was Dede's disability in *Between Friends* (Garrigue)? What did Ramona do to stop her father's smoking in *Ramona and Her Father* (Cleary)? Students often become insistent about verifying factual informa-tion by looking up specific passages in the book to prove their point.

More important, the motivation of different characters can be explored together, sometimes through students' projecting their own experiences into the story. Students can discuss why Carlie's attitude changed in *The Pinballs* (Byars), and speculate about how Harvey and Thomas J.'s actions helped break through her wall of defenses. They can debate why Jill remained loyal to Dede in *Between Friends* (Garrigue), and what they themselves would do if they were forced to choose between the in-crowd and a friendship with a girl who was retarded. Group discussion of a shared novel can help everyone, including the teacher and librarian, develop a deeper understanding of both the author's perspective and each reader's response to the text.

The Value of Realistic Fiction

In Project Equal, we use realistic contemporary fiction because the problems and issues the characters confront are similar to those that young adolescents experience every day. In these novels, acceptance by peers, changing family relationships, and identity questions are reflected through the eyes of girls and boys from different neighborhoods, different families, and different perspectives.

In contrast, folk tales and fantasy not only transport us away from our immediate environment into other times and other worlds but also often require the reader to deal with complex metaphors, abstract concepts, and figurative language. Realistic fiction is grounded in a more familiar and concrete reality and allows young adolescents to confront developmental issues more directly, expanding their understanding of the breadth of the human experience in the process.

The choice of realistic fiction as the literary foundation of Project Equal also rests on the following assumptions about motivating and broadening young readers.

1. *Children read differently when they read for pleasure than when they read to gain information.* In a motivational reading program such as Project Equal, children read novels for pleasure because they become involved with a story and a group of characters and want to know what happens to them. Some children may choose a book at first to please the teacher or librarian, or because their friends are reading the same book. Whatever the initial motive, they must become engaged with a book in order to sustain the reading and complete it.

   In this type of reading, termed "aesthetic" reading by Rosenblatt,[10] the reader experiences the story as an end in itself, rather than as a means to an end, usually the acquisition of factual information. The focus is on what is created during the reading—the feelings, ideas, and attitudes evoked by the book. Reading for pleasure enables children to "get lost in a book," enveloped in the action and the lives of the characters. Some students have reported missing their bus stop or "tuning out" their mother's voice because they were so engrossed in the novel they were reading.

   Reading for pleasure is more successful when children are allowed to choose the book they would like to read. Sometimes classroom teachers assign a book to a particular child, judging that he or she will not be able to complete a book chosen independently. Language arts teachers at the middle school or junior high level may be accustomed to studying a novel chapter by chapter as a class. Even librarians may attempt to discourage a child from selecting a particular novel because of the difficulty level or subject matter.

Yet in a motivational reading program that emphasizes reading for pleasure, students often find a way to complete books that are "too hard" or above their independent reading level if they are motivated enough by the story line and characterizations to keep reading. One student in Project Equal finished the book *Scorpions* (Myers) by reading with his mother at home because he desperately wanted to find out if Jamal joined the gang against his friend Tito's wishes. Some seventh and eighth grade boys have confessed that the Project Equal novel *Shadow Like a Leopard* (Levoy) was the first book they had ever completed on their own.

2. *Children need ready access to a variety of novels that address their developmental needs.* Schlager found that the most popular Newbery award–winning novels were those that featured developmental issues that are important to older children and young adolescents, such as developing friendships and striving for independence from adults.[11] Students may vary greatly from each other in their emotional and developmental needs. One student, feeling conflicted about his parents' recent divorce, may want to read *Dear Mr. Henshaw* (Cleary). Another may be quiet and shy and identify with Daphne, an outsider in *Daphne's Book* (Hahn). On the other hand, some students may want to vicariously experience a lifestyle and neighborhood very different from their own, such as Jess's experiences living on a farm in rural Maryland in *Bridge to Terabithia* (Paterson).

To provide the "right book for the right child at the right time," multiple copies of several different titles on a theme should be available so that every student can select a book that speaks to his or her needs at that time. Once completing a novel, students should be able to check out another book immediately, without having to wait until the next scheduled library period. If they aren't engaged with a book after reading two or three chapters, they should be able to exchange it for another one.

In Project Equal, we use the paperback editions of novels when available because we have found that young adolescents much prefer paperbacks for independent reading. When a particular title has not proved popular in the hard cover edition, readership has often dramatically increased when the paperback format was introduced.

3. *Children can identify with a fictional character like themselves.* Research on reader response indicates that while students may be reluctant to discuss personal experiences in the larger class, they identify with and will discuss in small groups fictional characters who embody similar problems and situations.[12] Students in Project Equal often comment in small group discussions and through journal writing activities how much they "feel" like a particular character. Children of color may see their lives reflected in a book for the first time. For example, a ten-year-old African American girl read *The Gift Giver* (Hansen) and commented on how much Doris's neighborhood and friends were like her own community. "I was never very

interested in reading, but now I want to read about what happens to Doris." She went on to eagerly read the sequel, *Yellow Bird and Me* (Hansen).

4. *Children can develop empathy with characters whose life experiences are different from their own.* In Katherine Paterson's words, "fiction allows us to do something that nothing else quite does. It allows us to enter fully into the lives of other human beings."[13] When students have the opportunity to share consciously in the life experiences of someone very different from themselves, they are able to empathize with a character and often gain new insights into others' attitudes and behaviors.

Some researchers on children's reading interests have found that boys prefer sports books and informational books about animals and science, while girls read more family stories and historical fiction with female characters.[14] In Project Equal we have found that both boys and girls will read realistic novels with female protagonists if the characters are depicted as interesting and active. There is little recent research on racial and ethnic reading preferences, but investigators in a 1971 study report that both white students and children of color prefer to read novels depicting their own racial group.[15] Although there appears to be some tendency for young adolescents to select novels reflecting their own experiences, we have discovered that students can be motivated to read about characters from backgrounds other than their own through book talks by teachers and library media specialists and recommendations from other students.

For example, sixth grade students in a predominantly white, working class neighborhood in Brooklyn were asked to keep a diary in the "voice" of their favorite character from a Project Equal book. Two white boys wrote perceptive diary entries in the voice of Doris from the book *Yellow Bird and Me* (Hansen), a novel set in a predominantly African American community in the Bronx (see example).

In another school, a Japanese American boy wrote a letter to the author of this book telling her how much he identified with Doris.

5. *Children's novels transmit values and perceptions of the world.* Historically, children's literature has been moralistic, designed to impart the "right" values and the socially accepted way to live. Meek points out how children's books have been determined by their social and historical context, and how what is produced and distributed influences what children read.[16] Segel discusses how nineteenth-century popular children's literature often focused on Christian moral tales with clearly defined gender roles for boys and girls.[17]

Today there is more variation in family styles, gender roles, and racial and cultural groups depicted in children's literature. Project Equal seeks out and highlights literature with diverse portrayals in family styles, gender roles, and the range of experiences in different racial and cultural communities. We focus on realistic juvenile novels that authentically depict

CHAPtER 3

THURSDAY 16	FRIDAY 17
Dear Diary, I got a job offer At the Bee Hive Salon. I would have to do extra things for Miss Bee and the other hair stylists. Like water the plant, take phone calls, clean the bottles, and more things. Now I have to ask my mother. I hope she says yes.	My father. I doubt he'll say no.
But if she dosen't say yes I'll ask	LATER ON
	in the day. I can't believe it. They're so unfair So stupid him and her won't let me work. What does she want me to do, the same thing. •she does. No way.

Fig. 1. Diary Entry

the experiences of children of color in the United States, as well as the experiences of recent immigrants from the Caribbean and Korea. Some novels are also included that depict the experiences of specific European

American groups, such as a Jewish American family in *Alan and Naomi* (Levoy) and Russian American immigrants in *Molly's Pilgrim* (Cohen). Novels chosen to portray a variety of white family styles include working-class families (*Dear Mr. Henshaw,* Cleary), middle-class families (*Maudie and Me and the Dirty Book,* Miles), and rural families (*Bridge to Terabithia,* Paterson and *Dicey's Song,* Voigt). A focus on realistic fiction sometimes limits the books that can be included in the program, because the literature available that depicts the experiences of some racial and ethnic groups, like native peoples, consists primarily of myths, legends, and folk tales.

Diversity in Project Equal Books

In Project Equal, we have found that presenting children with realistic fiction depicting a variety of racial/cultural groups, gender roles, and family styles enables them to both identify with characters like themselves and empathize with characters from different cultural perspectives. This literature can serve as an effective way to become aware of stereotypes and reduce prejudice.

How does literature with diverse portrayals of racial/cultural groups, gender roles, and family styles help children understand more about the diverse society in which they live? What are the aspects of the literature used in Project Equal that distinguish it from other children's literature?

1. *Language Differences*

   Language can influence concepts, interactions, and perceptions of the world. In *The Friends* (Guy), a teenager who has recently emigrated from the Caribbean struggles to make friends and confront her own class prejudices. The dialogue accurately reflects both the West Indian speech patterns of Phyllisia and her family and the African American English of her Harlem classmates. Characters in the book *Felita* (Mohr) incorporate both English and Spanish in their conversations, depicting one communication style in the Puerto Rican community in New York City. Although all of the books used in Project Equal are in English, a variety of ways of speaking English in the United States are represented. The author's effectiveness in capturing the dialogue between characters becomes a way of transmitting the distinctive aspects of the culture for the reader. Students from the community portrayed in a particular book can discuss if the characters sound real. "Is this the way kids you know really talk?" Children from other racial and cultural groups are exposed to different styles of communicating in a positive light.

   A fifth grader, a Puerto Rican girl, commented on how Felita's family talks the way her family does. "We talk in both Spanish and English at home." Discussing the sequel *Going Home* (Mohr), a seventh grade girl living in West Harlem talked about her feeling of discomfort when she went back to the Dominican Republic to visit relatives. "It was just like Felita. Kids made fun of my Spanish and said I talked with an accent."

Despite the occasional reservations of teachers and librarians, students in Project Equal generally have not had difficulty reading novels that incorporate different dialects in culturally appropriate contexts. For instance, although the use of African American English in children's books is still controversial, Wolfram points out that there is a "well established literary tradition of dialect representation for the benefit of the reader who may identify with the dialect."[18] We have found that portraying the way diverse characters really talk can help all children enter more fully into their lives and understand their perspectives.

2. *A Sense of Place*

All good literature has the ability to transport the reader and to give him or her the sense of "being there," watching the action take place. Multicultural literature should convey not only the scenery but also the unique aspects of the setting that are specific to that culture. A young teenage girl describes the sights and sounds of her East Harlem neighborhood in the coming-of-age novel *Nilda* (Mohr). *A Jar of Dreams* (Uchida) depicts the rural and small town life of Japanese Americans in California during the Depression.

To dispel stereotypes a variety of settings for each racial or cultural group should be highlighted. For instance, the African American experience in the United States spans urban, suburban, and rural settings and different class backgrounds. By reading *Justin and the Best Biscuits in the World* (Walter), students learn about the role of black cowboys and homesteaders in the settlement of the West through Justin's adventures on his grandfather's ranch in Missouri. *Charlie Pippin* (Boyd) depicts a young adolescent's experiences growing up in a middle-class family in Berkeley, California, and her efforts to come to terms with her father's involvement in the Vietnam War. In *Roll of Thunder, Hear My Cry* (Taylor), the reader experiences both the warmth and the cohesiveness of a rural African American southern community of the 1930s, as well as the impact of racism and segregation on that community.

Such books give an insider's view of the community where the story takes place and provide enough specific details to give the reader a sense of what makes this place distinctive. Questions a teacher or librarian can ask include: Can you imagine what this community looks like? Do the descriptions make you feel you are a part of the community, even though you may never have visited a place like this?

Children who have lived in similar communities see their experiences validated in literature. "Did this really happen?" or "Does this story take place on 125th Street? It seems so much like my neighborhood," they may say. For students from different backgrounds, an insider's perspective provides them with a viewpoint they may have never considered and the opportunity to experience both the uniqueness of another culture and the universality of the human experience. Students comment that they "didn't know it was like that" in response to the legal segregation depicted in Mildred Taylor's books set in the South, or remark that "Charlie's family is just like mine" after reading about her experiences with sibling rivalry in *Charlie Pippin* (Boyd).

3. *Family Relationships*

Most juvenile novels depict a central family or families around which the action revolves. Increasingly, as our society experiences a variety of family styles and configurations, the families in juvenile novels have become more diverse. A novel used in Project Equal might show family patterns and interactions that are specific to particular cultural groups. For instance, Felita's extended family forms an important link with her family's past in Puerto Rico and her current life in New York City.

Abuelita is a confidante who reminds Felita to be proud of her history and her heritage in *Felita* (Mohr). Tio Jorge facilitates her trip to Puerto Rico for the summer in *Going Home* (Mohr), enabling her to begin to resolve some identity questions in this coming-of-age story. Casey's grandmother also serves as an important source of information and support in formulating her cultural identity as a Chinese American in the book *Child of the Owl* (Yep).

In today's society there is a diversity of family styles that spans different cultures and communities. Single-parent families, foster families, homeless families, gay families, and "blended" families that bring together children from previous marriages are becoming increasingly common. Although the traditional nuclear family still predominates in juvenile fiction, some contemporary novels have begun to reflect the current reality of family life in the United States.

In *The Great Gilly Hopkins* (Paterson), a rebellious foster child must face the realization that her dream of returning to live with her "natural" mother won't come true, but that her foster family can provide her with the love she needs. In *Ramona and Her Father* (Cleary), Ramona must adjust to her mother's return to full-time work when her father loses his job. Leigh in *Dear Mr. Henshaw* (Cleary) resents his father's absence after his parents divorce, but he begins to come to terms with his feelings and establish a place in both of their lives in the sequel *Strider* (Cleary). December, a homeless girl who has run away from an abusive foster family in *Sam and the Moon Queen* (Herzig and Mali), creates her own "family" through her relationship with Annie, an older homeless woman, and Sam, a new boy in the neighborhood. Project Equal novels are selected to depict both the uniqueness and the commonalities of family relationships in different cultures, communities, and settings, showing not only the struggles and difficulties but also the love, understanding, and support to be found in all kinds of families.

4. *Gender Roles*

Historically, the depiction of female roles in juvenile fiction has been limited to traditional portrayals of girls and women in nurturing and supportive roles, often dependent on the evaluations of others for their identity. There have always been notable exceptions, such as Caddie in *Caddie Woodlawn* (Brink), Jo in *Little Women* (Alcott), or Laura in the "Little House" books by Laura Ingalls Wilder, but the message even in these books has been that spirited and independent girls "settle down" by young adulthood and become wives and mothers whose lives are focused around their families.

In Project Equal, we feature books that include a range of portrayals of girls from different racial and cultural groups who are adventurous and courageous, seeking to control their own destinies, as well as books that portray females in nurturing roles. Ramona, the protagonist in *Ramona and Her Mother* (Cleary) and *Ramona and Her Father* (Cleary), is an adventurous young girl who is always getting in trouble in these warm family stories for younger readers. Twelve-year-old Julilly in *Runaway to Freedom* (Smucker) helps her friend Liza escape from a Southern plantation on the Underground Railroad to Canada and freedom. With courage and determination she takes charge of her life. In *The House on Mango Street* (Cisneros), an episodic novel for older readers, Esperanza dreams of a "house of my own . . . Not a man's house. Not a daddy's. A house all my own. . . ." The narrator, growing up in a Latino community in Chicago, begins to define her own identity as a young woman in this coming-of-age story.

Males have also traditionally been depicted in limited roles in juvenile fiction. They have been allowed to be adventurous and courageous but have been denied their nurturing and expressive qualities. In Project Equal novels boys are shown displaying their vulnerability and emotions, often by engaging in such creative activities as drawing or writing. Alfie, a quiet artist in *The Cartoonist* (Byars), is devastated when he learns his older brother and his wife plan to move back and live in Alfie's attic retreat. Jess, another talented artist in *Bridge to Terabithia* (Paterson), struggles with his father's disapproval of his art work and develops a close friendship with an athletic, nonconformist girl, despite the taunts of his classmates. Ramon in *Shadow Like a Leopard* (Levoy) is afraid to let the other gang members know he writes poetry for fear of being labeled a "sissy."

Depicting a range of gender roles in juvenile fiction provides young adolescents with diverse role models with which to identify. It also confirms that there is no one way to be "male" or "female" in our society, but a variety of human attributes and qualities that may be present in any individual.

5. *Themes of Prejudice and Discrimination*

Several researchers have commented that incidents and experiences of prejudice and discrimination are often depicted in multicultural fiction. Sims notes that the will and strength to survive oppression and other hardships is a common theme in African American literature.[19] Carver also found this theme prevalent in literature depicting Native Americans.[20] Romero and Zancanella noted the same emphasis in their review of Hispanic literature.[21]

Project Equal novels generally depict prejudice and discrimination from the perspective of the group being discriminated against. For example, in the book *The Gold Cadillac* (Taylor), an African American family living in Toledo, Ohio, in 1950 drives their new car south to visit relatives in Mississippi. The reader experiences racism firsthand when the father is stopped by a white police officer, arrested, and held for several hours in the police station merely because the officer doesn't believe they own the car. During the trip, the two young girls in the family are exposed to legal segregation for the first time when they stop to get gas and cannot use the "white" drinking fountain. A significant aspect of this book is that the reader experiences the full emotional impact of racism, as if he or she were there. Taylor's ability to convey the insider's perspective makes it a powerful book and enables the reader to empathize effectively with the characters.

The Gold Cadillac was read aloud to a seventh grade class. During the class discussion following the reading, the Project Equal facilitator asked, "Do you think something like this could happen today?" An African American boy responded, "Yes, my cousin was stopped by the police and questioned for no reason." The teacher spontaneously related a personal story illustrating this point. "My husband, a black professional, was stopped one day while driving our BMW. The police said they thought he was a drug dealer." A candid discussion ensued about possible stereotypes the police might have about African American men.

An understanding of racial prejudice and discrimination can help students identify parallel examples of unequal treatment in literature. When asked to describe characters in Project Equal books who experienced prejudice, students not only discussed books that depict racial prejudice, such as *Felita* (Mohr) or *The Gold Cadillac* (Taylor); they also pointed to Dede in *Between Friends* (Garrigue) who was teased because she was retarded and Barbara Fisher in *The Real Me* (Miles), who was not allowed to take over her brother's paper route because she was a girl. Students begin to understand the complexity of issues of diversity and the need to be sensitive to all types of inequities.

To implement a thematically organized literature program, a collection of high quality multicultural fiction must be developed. What criteria are important in the selection process? How can the library media specialist and the classroom teacher work together to develop a collection that meets the needs of their students? Chapter 4 will discuss expanded selection criteria and the collaborative process of building a collection of multicultural literature that emphasizes diversity.

Notes

1. Joyce Carol Oates, in *The Reader's Quotation Book: A Literary Companion,* ed. Steven Gilbar (New York: Penguin Books, 1991), 16.

2. Charlotte Huck, "I Give You the End of a Golden String," *Theory into Practice* 21 (Autumn 1982): 315–321.

3. Louise M. Rosenblatt, *The Reader, The Text, The Poem* (Carbondale: Southern Illinois University Press, 1978).

4. Susan I. Hepler and Janet Hickman, "'The Book Was Okay I Love You'—Social Aspects of Response to Literature," *Theory into Practice* 21 (Autumn 1982): 278–283.

5. James Flood and Diane Lapp, "Research and Practice: A Reader Response Approach to the Teaching of Literature," *Reading Research and Instruction* 27 (Summer 1988): 61–66.

6. Rudine Sims, "Strong Black Girls: A Ten Year Old Responds to Fiction about Afro-Americans," *Journal of Research and Development in Education* 16 (Spring 1983): 21–28.

7. Lorraine Foreman-Peck, "Evaluating Children's Talk about Literature: A Theoretical Perspective," *Children's Literature in Education* 16 (Winter 1985): 203–218.

8. Joanne M. Golden, "Reader-Text Interaction," *Theory into Practice* 25 (Spring 1986): 91–96.

9. Maryann Eeds and Deborah Wells, "Grand Conversations: An Exploration of Meaning Construction in Literature Study Groups," *Research in the Teaching of English* 23 (Feb. 1989): 4–29.

10. Louise M. Rosenblatt, "The Literary Transaction: Evocation and Response," *Theory into Practice* 21 (Autumn 1982): 268–277.

11. Norma Schlager, "Predicting Children's Choices in Literature: A Developmental Approach," *Children's Literature in Education* 9 (Autumn 1978): 136–142.

12. Alan C. Purves and Richard Beach, *Literature and the Reader: Research in Response to Literature, Reading Interests, and the Teaching of Literature* (Urbana, Ill.: National Council of Teachers of English, 1972).

13. Katherine Paterson, *Gates of Excellence: On Reading and Writing Books for Children* (New York: Elsener/Nelson Books, 1981), 58.

14. Deborah Langerman, "Books and Boys: Gender Preferences and Book Selection," *School Library Journal* 36 (March 1990): 132–136.

15. Sarah Elizabeth Barchas, "Expressed Reading Interests of Children of Differing Ethnic Groups" (Ph.D. diss., Univ. of Arizona, 1971).

16. Margaret Meek, "What Counts as Evidence in Theories of Children's Literature?" *Theory into Practice* 21 (Autumn 1982): 284–292.

17. Elizabeth Segel, "'As the Twig is Bent . . .': Gender and Childhood Reading," in *Gender and Reading: Essays on Readers, Texts, and Contexts,* ed. Elizabeth A. Flynn and Patrocinio P. Schweickart (Baltimore: John Hopkins University Press, 1986), 165–186.

18. Walt Wolfram, *Dialects and American English* (Englewood Cliffs, N.J.: Prentice-Hall, 1991), 256.

19. Rudine Sims, *Shadow and Substance: Afro-American Experience in Contemporary Fiction* (Urbana, Ill.: National Council of Teachers of English, 1982).

20. Nancy Lynn Carver, "Stereotypes of American Indians in Adolescent Literature," *English Journal* 77 (Sept. 1988): 25–31.

21. Patricia Ann Romero and Don Zancanella, "Expanding the Circle: Hispanic Voices in American Literature," *English Journal* 79 (Jan. 1990): 24–29.

References

Alcott, Louisa May. *Little Women.* Boston: Little, Brown, 1915.

Brink, Carol Ryrie. *Caddie Woodlawn.* New York: Macmillan, 1935.

Wilder, Laura Ingalls. *Little House in the Big Woods.* New York: Harper & Row, 1932.

———. *Little House on the Prairie.* New York: Harper & Row, 1935.

4

Multicultural Literature: The Selection Process

We read for delight. But at the same time we must read with a discerning eye and mind, with the intention of defining that delight . . . that means going beyond our emotional reaction to a critical analysis of the book.

Elizabeth Fitzgerald Howard
"Delight and Definition:
The Nuts and Bolts of Evaluating
Children's Books"[1]

The books that reach children should authentically depict and interpret their lives and their history, build self-respect and encourage the development of positive values, make children aware of their strength and leave them with a sense of hope and direction.

Eloise Greenfield
"Writing for Children: A Joy
and a Responsibility"[2]

Literary Quality and Values: A Balancing Act

The selection process for a multicultural literature-based program challenges teachers and library media specialists to critically examine contemporary realistic fiction. Literary quality is an important criterion, of course, but so are the values and perspectives conveyed by the book. Also, as a motivational reading program, Project Equal must include books that address student interests and developmental needs. The objectives of the program—to promote diversity and critical reading abilities—must be balanced with the needs and interests of the students. Questions that arise in the selection process include: Should I concentrate on books that I think will be popular with my students? Or should I include books most students wouldn't pick up on their own, titles that expose them to diverse communities and new experiences? How should literary quality be weighted in comparison with criteria that address social and ethical values, including cultural diversity?

In Project Equal we consider several criteria before including a realistic novel as part of the program. First of all, we examine the overall literary quality, with an eye to how questions of cultural authenticity and diverse family and gender roles may influence the perspective of the book. Then we look at readability and the interest the book may have for young adolescent readers in an urban environment. Finally, we discuss possible stereotypes in the book and decide whether the positive aspects of the book outweigh whatever negative portrayals may be present.

Three questions outlined by Purves and Monson that we find helpful when judging realistic fiction for literary merit are "Does the book succeed in arousing my emotions?" "Is the book well written?" and "Is the book meaningful?"[3] Questions of literary quality are examined with a particular focus on the importance of authenticity in multicultural fiction.

"Does the Book Succeed in Arousing My Emotions?"

Do you find yourself laughing or crying while reading the book? Are you sorry to put the book down after it's over? One teacher in Project Equal reported to his sixth grade class that he cried four times while reading *Alan and Naomi* (Levoy), the story of a friendship between a Jewish American teenager and an emotionally troubled refugee from Nazi-occupied Europe. Books that produce a valid emotional response hold up over time and produce a similar response on the second or third reading. They will also engender a similar response in children, if the difficulty level and author's style are accessible. *Bridge to Terabithia* (Paterson) is a favorite with teachers and library media specialists in the program because of the emotional depth of the book. This book has been less popular with some of the students, however, perhaps because the complexity of the language makes it more difficult for them to tap into the emotional experience.

"Is the Book Well Written?"

This second question posed by Purves and Monson judges the quality of the writing and can be addressed by examining such traditional literary elements as setting, point of view, characterizations, plot, theme, and style. Each of these elements takes on a distinctive meaning in the evaluation of multicultural fiction that emphasizes diversity.

SETTING

The setting of a novel includes both the geographical location and the time in which the story takes place. Arbuthnot and Sutherland state that the setting should be "clear, believable, and authentic."[4] Details of the setting should be included in a casual, natural way, described through the dialogue and interwoven into the action.

In multicultural fiction the setting will vary, but it should "ring true" for the families and the racial and cultural communities featured in a particular novel. *Child of the Owl* (Yep) evokes the sights and sounds of San Francisco's Chinatown neighborhood. *A Jar of Dreams* (Uchida) depicts the lives of Japanese American farmers in rural California in the 1930s. *Scorpions* (Myers) places the reader on the streets of contemporary Harlem. When selecting fiction for Project Equal, we try to include a range of settings—rural, suburban, and urban—that feature the experiences of different racial and cultural groups.

Many multicultural books, especially those depicting the lives of African American children, are set in urban neighborhoods. This setting may provide a familiar backdrop for the New York City students in Project Equal, but it does not reflect the lives of the African American children throughout the country who live in rural areas, small towns, and suburban communities. A book like *Justin and the Best Biscuits in the World* (Walter) helps diversify the depiction of the African American experience and introduces students to the role of black cowboys and homesteaders in the settlement of the Midwest.

POINT OF VIEW

Who tells the story? Is there an omniscient narrator who simply describes the characters, or does the protagonist tell the story and the reader see the characters only through the narrator's eyes? If the author tells the story in the first person, he or she must be sufficiently familiar with the language patterns and perspective of someone from that particular culture and background to create believable characters and dialogue. The author's background and perspective continue to be controversial issues in multicultural fiction. Such scholars as Rudine Sims Bishop argue that a writer who is not from the same cultural background as the protagonist is more likely to write from an outsider's point of view, while an author from the culture will write from an insider's perspective.[5] Children's book authors Belinda Hurmence and Paula Fox assert that good writers can transcend their background and use their imagination to realistically portray a character with very different life experiences from their own.[6]

In Project Equal we generally select realistic fiction from an insider's perspective, usually written by authors from the racial and cultural backgrounds and communities they depict. We have found that stories told from an insider's perspective more accurately reflect the nuances of everyday life in that community. They are also more likely to engender an emotional response in children and identification with the characters, perhaps because they place the reader "inside" the action, viewing events through the characters' eyes. Novels depicting an insider's perspective are often less likely to contain racial stereotypes, although they may still contain limited portrayals of gender roles and family styles.

Someone who is not from a particular cultural background or community may be able to write convincingly from an insider's perspective if he or she is sufficiently familiar with the language patterns and social relationships in that community. A writer may be able to capture the flavor of a particular historical period, for instance, by researching oral histories, diary entries, and eyewitness accounts. Hansen argues, however, that perspective is critical in historical fiction, and that the writer must be aware that historical accounts were often influenced by the perspective of the historian and the prevailing social and political attitudes at the time the accounts were recorded.[7] Occasionally we have included historical fiction written by an author whose background differs from that of the characters, such as *Runaway to Freedom* (Smucker), the story of two girls who escape slavery to Canada on the Underground Railroad during the 1850s, and *A Girl Called Boy* (Hurmence), the story of a contemporary African American girl who is transported into the pre–Civil War South and experiences slavery first hand.

How do teachers and library media specialists know whether the point of view of a novel "rings true" or whether the dialogue between characters and the details of everyday life are accurately portrayed? Before including a book in a multicultural literature–based program, consult critical reviews of the book in annotated bibliographies and professional journals to find out about questions of authenticity, or ask other colleagues to read and comment on it, especially those who may be more familiar with the cultural backgrounds and lifestyles of the characters. In Project Equal, we often ask several teachers and library media specialists to read and discuss a novel before we include it in the program.

CHARACTERIZATION

How believable are the characters? Do they grow and change naturally as a result of events in the story? Do the characterizations show depth, or are they one-dimensional portraits that border on caricatures? Examining characterization goes to the heart of selecting literature that promotes diversity. Characters who lack depth and believability often reinforce societal stereotypes and provide students with inaccurate or incomplete pictures of a particular racial or cultural community. Complex portrayals that show a range of human responses and emotions can help dispel stereotypes and encourage students to identify and empathize with the characters.

We ask a number of questions when examining characterizations in realistic fiction. Is there a range of family roles portrayed in a particular novel? Are all families other than the traditional nuclear family shown as dysfunctional, or are there single-parent families, foster families, and extended families depicted that are loving and supportive? In realistic fiction, family problems are often critical to the plot and the theme of the book. However, novels that portray only a negative view of family life in a particular racial or cultural community may inadvertently reinforce stereotypes.

Does the reader get a sense of the variety of perspectives and lifestyles present in a particular neighborhood and racial/cultural community? In the African American neighborhood depicted in Chicago in *Forever Friends* (Boyd), Project

Equal students are introduced to Tony, a serious girl whose professional parents pressure her to achieve academically; her fun-loving friend, Susan, who lives with her rather straitlaced grandparents; and sensitive but self-sufficient Raymond, who lives with his mother in a nearby housing project. In the multiracial Berkeley neighborhood of *Charlie Pippin* (Boyd), a later novel by the same author, Chartreuse's African American extended family includes her traditional, middle-class parents; her free-spirited grandmother who takes her to a peace demonstration; Uncle Ben, a Vietnam veteran; and Aunt Jessie, an independent working woman who lives alone in Washington, D.C. Depicting a variety of lifestyles in a particular racial or cultural community helps the reader gain insight into the diversity present in that community.

Another area we examine when looking at characterizations is the portrayal of gender roles. Are the girls and women in the novel shown as adventurous and self-sufficient, able to solve problems on their own? Although there is still a shortage of active, competent girls in contemporary realistic fiction, girls are still often depicted in a greater variety of roles than are adult women. Two Project Equal books that depict the growth and change of both a girl and her mother are *Ramona and Her Father* (Cleary) and *Ramona and Her Mother* (Cleary). Ramona is shown as lively and mischievous. Her mother is depicted in a more traditional nurturing role, although she goes back to work full time when her husband loses his job. In the sequel, Ramona's mother reveals that she likes working and that she will continue in her job after Ramona's father is reemployed. The episode in the book in which Ramona's mother and father arrive home to an uncooked dinner and argue over who forgot to plug in the crockpot is one of the more memorable and realistic scenes featuring working parents in contemporary juvenile fiction.

Are the male characters shown as expressive and sensitive, depicted in nurturing roles as well as more traditional male roles? Jamal in *Scorpions* (Myers) is a sensitive artist, challenging the stereotype of a tough inner-city kid who gets involved with a gang. Examples of adult men in nurturing roles include Justin's grandfather who takes care of him for the summer, teaching him how to cook and clean house in *Justin and the Best Biscuits in the World* (Walter), and Mr. Mason in *The Pinballs* (Byars), who comforts Thomas J. upon the death of the Benson twins and helps him understand the importance of expressing his feelings.

INTERACTIONS BETWEEN CHARACTERS

The relationships between characters represent another important aspect to examine when selecting multicultural fiction. Are male and female characters shown as friends and equals, or are young adolescent girls depicted as "boy crazy," needing a boyfriend to make their lives complete and give their lives meaning? Project Equal books are chosen to highlight the possibility and importance of friendships between females and males. Sam and December in *Sam and*

the Moon Queen (Herzig and Mali), Doris and Amir in *The Gift Giver* (Hansen), Alan and Naomi in *Alan and Naomi* (Levoy), and Jess and Leslie in *Bridge to Terabithia* (Paterson) demonstrate that boys and girls can relate to each other with trust and respect.

Are people of color shown as capable of solving their own problems, or is a benevolent white character introduced to save the day? Walter Dean Myers, in an interview with Rudine Sims Bishop, points out the lack of realistic juvenile fiction that shows African American characters helping each other: "A white can help a white; a black can help a white, but a black cannot help a black. I find that a very precious relationship, so I want to put that in my books."[8] In his novel *Won't Know Till I Get There* (Myers), a middle-class African American family becomes a foster family to a street-wise, African American adolescent.

PLOT

What happens in the story? The plot of the story involves a series of actions that takes a character through time and change. We ask the following questions about plot to help us through the selection process: Does the sequence of events seem realistic? Does the story hold my attention? Does the ending make sense based on the characters' change and development, or are the plot strands wrapped up too neatly?

Some books for children and young adolescents provide an artificially happy ending at odds with real life. Project Equal books have been selected for their realistic depictions of problems young people face in contemporary American society. In *Dear Mr. Henshaw* (Cleary), Leigh's divorced parents do not reunite, and he must learn to adjust to life alone with his mother and in a new school and community. In *Felita* (Mohr), the overt discrimination the Maldonado family experiences from their new neighbors does not end, and Felita's family decides to move back to their old neighborhood.

We believe that while realistic fiction for young adolescents should mirror real life, it should not be overly depressing or fatalistic. Young people need stories that not only explore life's problems but also provide insight into those problems and hope for the future. Books should be selected to highlight the resiliency of the human spirit. Neil's father moves to his own apartment in *Welcome Home Jellybean* (Shyer), unable to cope with the day-to-day reality of living with a severely retarded daughter. At the end of the story, there is no guarantee that his father will return, but Neil has grown in compassion and self-knowledge and the reader is assured that he will be able to handle the challenges life presents.

•

THEME

What is the main idea of the story? What is the author's perception of the human experience? We agree with Arbuthnot and Sutherland that an implicit theme that is intrinsic to the story is more effective than a didactic "message" book.[9] An engaging novel envelops the reader in the actions and thoughts of the characters. Awareness of the theme comes after finishing the book, when the reader reflects on the story as a whole.

There are many possible themes that can be explored in a literature-based program for young adolescents. Zingher describes how such themes as bullies and villains, survival, and humor can be implemented with older children in the library media program.[10] In Project Equal we select books that feature such developmental themes as peer friendship, family relationships, self-awareness, and prejudice and discrimination. These are recurring themes in realistic multicultural fiction that we have found to be popular with the ten- to fourteen-year-old students in our program and resonate with their developmental needs.

Exploring these themes through multicultural novels provides students with fictional role models and information about how other families and communities resolve problems and conflicts. Students can compare and contrast both the universal elements and the specific cultural differences in the depiction of a theme once several novels have been read.

When selecting novels on the theme of peer friendship and peer pressure, for instance, one should look for books that explore such common adolescent problems as exclusion, name calling, loyalty, and pressure to conform. We look for books that explore the complexities of a theme in a naturalistic way and speak to the situations that young adolescents face in their everyday lives. Often a Project Equal book features a character who stands up for someone who has been excluded or resists peer pressure. In *Between Friends* (Garrigue), Jill chooses to go to a party with her friend Dede, who has Down syndrome, rather than a dance performance with the more popular students. Edith, in the book *The Friends* (Guy), defends Phyllisia from other students in her class who perceive her as "uppity" and taunt her about her accent and West Indian ancestry.

Characters in good books don't always "do the right thing" and speak up when another character is ostracized or experiences prejudice. Jessica in *Daphne's Book* (Hahn) has several moments when she distances herself from Daphne, unsure if she is willing to risk teasing and exclusion by maintaining her friendship with an outsider. Her loyalty to Daphne is further tested when she must decide if she will break her promise and reveal Daphne's problems.

STYLE

How is the story written? How are the ideas expressed? Thrall, Hibbard, and Holman note, in *A Handbook to Literature,* that "the best style for any given purpose is that which most nearly approximates a perfect adaptation of one's language to one's ideas."[11] In multicultural fiction the style should be appropriate to the story and the setting, with realistic dialogue that conveys authentic speech patterns. For inclusion in a literature-based program, a novel should have a style accessible not only to readers from the cultural tradition depicted but also to readers from other backgrounds who may be unfamiliar with the setting and verbal interactions. If the narrator or one or more characters in the novel incorporate language other than standard English, the dialogue should be realistic but readable. Joyce Hansen and Walter Dean Myers are two authors of novels for young adolescents who capture the uniqueness and richness of language styles in African American communities through dialogue that we have found understandable to all children.

"Is the Book Meaningful?"

Purves and Monson's last question for judging literary merit refers to the writer's seriousness and the importance of the issues raised in the book. Some juvenile fiction presents a facile treatment of developmental issues for young adolescents, a kind of "situation comedy" approach to friendships and family life in which characters act in predictable ways and the ambiguities of life are superficially explored. In Project Equal we look for realistic fiction that presents a serious look at such critical contemporary issues as self-pride, standing up for one's beliefs, respecting differences, and promoting equality. We look for books that explore these issues from the child's perspective in everyday scenarios where children must make decisions about whom to befriend or how to respond to family problems.

By its very nature multicultural literature deals with serious issues because it portrays the history and experiences of all Americans, not just those who have traditionally been in the mainstream. It is how those experiences are depicted, however, that determines the novel's depth of meaning. Are conflicts minimized or explored? Are historical instances of racism and discrimination glossed over or presented realistically in a way that an older child or young adolescent can understand? In *Journey to Topaz* (Uchida) and *Journey Home* (Uchida), the reader experiences the harshness of the Japanese American internment camps during World War II and the subsequent racism Yuki and her family face when they return home to Berkeley and their store is burned. These negative realities, however, are presented in the context of a warm and supportive extended family life that nurtures Yuki and sustains her belief in herself. Multicultural literature that explores not only the positive values of family and community life but also the negative effects of prejudice and discrimination helps children understand the impact of inequality on individuals and communities.

Readability and Interest

Will the students we know like and read this book? After considering questions of literary quality and authenticity, before including a new novel as part of Project Equal we look at student interest. We have found that if a book is too long (more than 250 pages), has too many descriptive passages, or contains too many abstract allusions, most young adolescents will not complete it independently. Sometimes we select a novel even though we know it won't be popular with the majority of students because it features nontraditional gender roles or depicts a unique cultural experience not represented by other books in the program. *Dicey's Song* (Voigt) has not been extremely popular with Project Equal students, probably because the length of the book and the descriptive style make it difficult for all but the best readers to complete. We include it, however, because of its strong portrait of an independent female who is coming of age and balancing issues of self-interest and commitment to family concerns. *Child of the Owl* (Yep) is another complex novel that is not widely read, but we include it as part of our program because it is one of the few books that depicts a Chinese American girl discovering and integrating her Chinese heritage with her present American reality.

Occasionally we include a novel on a trial basis for a year to assess student interest and issues raised in small group discussions. *Sidewalk Story* (Mathis) was added to Project Equal this year when it was reissued in paperback format after being out of print for several years. This short novella concerns Lily Etta's fight to help her friend Tanya and her family, who have been evicted. Although intended for younger readers, the book has proved its appeal and usefulness for young adolescents because it's easy to read, emotionally satisfying, and raises important class issues about the differential treatment of poor people.

The Selection Process

Where do library media specialists and teachers find high quality, multicultural literature that promotes diversity? Once you locate books that might be appropriate, how do you determine questions of authenticity? Miller-Lachman summarizes the history of multicultural publishing in the United States in her comprehensive multicultural bibliography.[12] After a decrease in the publishing of multicultural literature in the 1980s, a renewed interest in multicultural issues in the 1990s has produced new bibliographies as well as a small increase in the publishing of multicultural, particularly African American, literature. Annotated topical bibliographies are one source of realistic fiction that emphasizes diversity. Library, language arts, and literature journals that publish book reviews are another. We agree with Arbuthnot and Sutherland, however, that "the best way to know books is to read them."[13] You can narrow down the field through reading others' reviews and annotations, but when selecting a collection of novels to be used in a library-classroom literature program, there is no substitute for reading and discussing potential books with your colleagues.

Examining Stereotypes

Just as different children respond differently to the same book, each adult reader has a unique response. In Project Equal we often find that project staff, library media specialists, and classroom teachers will differ in their responses to the same book. Sometimes school staff will point out what they perceive as a stereotyped portrayal in a Project Equal book and question why we have included the book in the program. We have found that adults are more likely to identify with the adult characters in the book and often respond negatively to limited or overly simplistic portrayals of parents or teachers. For example, some teachers and library media specialists have pointed to the negative portrayal of Alfie's mother in *The Cartoonist* (Byars). She continually watches game shows on television and implies that Alfie should be more like his older brother, Bubba, an outgoing and popular young man who often gets in trouble in school. Alfie, the protagonist, is a quiet boy who feels alienated from his family and prefers drawing alone in his attic retreat. Alfie's mother *is* stereotypically portrayed, but the central theme of the book is Alfie's plight to find a "room of his own," to be himself and pursue his own interests away from the shadow of his brother. Alfie becomes the role model for boys who feel their concerns and talents don't fit into the traditional male mold. Rather than rejecting the book, the limited portrayal of Alfie's mother can be discussed and debated with readers in the book discussion format. The positive aspects of this book outweigh any negative effects of the stereotyped portrayals of the adults.

Subtle racial stereotypes may also be explored in book conversations between staff members. Someone with an "insider's" perspective may have a perception of a book that differs from that of a colleague who is not from the racial or cultural community depicted. One African American teacher in Project Equal recently stated that she felt Angie's shoplifting at the end of the book *The Shimmershine Queens* (Yarbrough) struck a false note and marred an otherwise authentic and interesting portrayal of an African American girl's development of pride in herself and her African heritage.

It is difficult if not impossible to develop a collection of multicultural literature that is totally free of stereotypes. Authors write from their own unique perspectives and create characters as part of a story, not based on a formula or checklist. Some novels present more multidimensional perspectives than others, however, or achieve more authenticity in the portrayal of the nuances of everyday interactions in particular communities. Creating multicultural diversity and balance in the total collection of novels included as part of a library-classroom literature-based program is more important than excluding an otherwise worthwhile book because of one stereotyped portrayal.

Book discussions between library media specialists and teachers, especially if they include staff from diverse backgrounds, help shed light on characterizations, emphasize positive and negative aspects of individual books, and reveal the types of books needed to provide balance in the literature-based program. We incorporate book discussions in our initial training sessions and then encourage teachers and library media specialists to discuss the books with each other during ongoing planning meetings throughout the program.

Maintaining a Critical Approach

After deciding which novels to include in a literature-based program, we encourage staff and students to continue the critical examination of characterizations and portrayals in the book discussion process. Staff and students have the opportunity to share their personal responses to books as well as to critique them in light of their increased awareness of issues of diversity as part of the ongoing program. Taking a critical approach to the novels used in Project Equal helps students develop critical reading skills and begin to formulate their own criteria for determining what is high-quality, nonstereotyped realistic fiction.

How do students develop greater understanding and acceptance of diversity? What kinds of activities help students relate the themes explored in multicultural fiction to real-life problems? The next chapter will illustrate how to integrate a multicultural literature-based program into the library media center and the classroom using the Project Equal thematic approach as a model.

Notes

1. Elizabeth Fitzgerald Howard, "Delight and Definition: The Nuts and Bolts of Evaluating Children's Books," *Top of the News* 43 (Summer 1987): 363.

2. Eloise Greenfield, "Writing for Children: A Joy and a Responsibility," in *The Black American in Books for Children: Readings in Racism,* 2d edition, ed. Donnarae McCann and Gloria Woodard (Metuchen, N.J.: Scarecrow Press, 1985), 21.

3. Alan C. Purves and Dianne L. Monson, *Experiencing Children's Literature* (Glenview, Ill.: Scott Foresman, 1984), 152.

4. May Arbuthnot and Zena Sutherland, *Children and Books,* 8th edition (New York: HarperCollins, 1991).

5. Rudine Sims, "A Question of Perspective," *The Advocate* 3 (Summer 1984): 145–156.

6. Belinda Hurmence, "Point of View: A Question of Perspective II & III," *The Advocate* 4 (Fall 1984): 20–23; Paula Fox, "To Write Simply," *Horn Book* (September/October 1991): 552–555.

7. Joyce Hansen, "Whose Story Is It?," *The New Advocate* 3 (Summer 1990): 167–173.

8. Rudine Sims Bishop, "Profile: Walter Dean Myers," *Language Arts* 67 (Dec. 1990): 866.

9. Arbuthnot and Sutherland, *Children and Books,* 43.

10. Gary Zingher, *At the Pirate Academy: Adventures with Language in the Library Media Center* (Chicago: American Library Association, 1990).

11. William Thrall, Addison Hibbard, and C. Hugh Holman, *A Handbook to Literature* (New York: Odyssey, 1960), 474.

12. Lyn Miller-Lachman, *Our Family, Our Friends, Our World: An Annotated Guide to Significant Multicultural Books for Children and Teenagers* (New York: Bowker, 1992), 9.

13. Arbuthnot and Sutherland, *Children and Books,* 36.

5

Implementing the Thematic Approach to Multicultural Literature

I admit that when my principal first approached me about participating in the program, I had my doubts. Yet . . . I found this to be one of the few innovative programs that we were able to continue on our own. It is a program that fosters library-classroom planning for the benefit of the language arts curriculum. I was able to model my future lessons after those which were so ably demonstrated.

> Binnie Meltzer
> Language Arts Teacher
> J.H.S. 189Q[1]

Although they had met the Project Equal facilitator during the all-day training sessions, the middle school teacher and library media specialist were clearly apprehensive. As they waited in the school library for the first planning meeting they wondered what was expected of them and how the facilitator would proceed. Was she going to model a lesson with the students? If so, could she handle discipline? Keep their attention? What kind of lesson would they begin with? How were the issues and themes mentioned in the workshops—understanding stereotypes, book themes, and independent reading—going to be integrated into the lessons they would be implementing?

The forty-minute planning meeting cleared up many of their concerns. Long-term goals were set, and the facilitator described the lesson she would model with assistance from the teacher and librarian who were familiar with the students and their work. Together they would begin with an introductory lesson on stereotyping.

Not until the lesson was over did the newly participating staff breathe with relief. The students had responded, the teaching team had worked together effectively. They began to look forward to the next sessions.

Introducing the Project: A Focus on Stereotypes

The students in the target class had responded eloquently when asked, "What does the word *stereotyping* mean to you?" By authority of their own experiences of bias and their observations of stereotypes in the media, in the school yard, and in the halls, *they* were treated as the experts with the information. The facilitator, assisted by the language arts teacher and the library media specialist, organized and summarized the responses into a definition of stereotyping, a listing of groups who experience prejudice in the United States, and a breakdown of the effects of both negative (all lawyers are dishonest) and positive (all Chinese are good at math) stereotypes. Students got a chance to think about common racial stereotypes and epithets as well as gender stereotypes. They saw how the facts—in this case statistics offered by the facilitator about women drivers—contradicted the stereotype some of them held. Students and staff listened carefully and responded to one another, one at a time.

This Project Equal lesson, based on open-ended questions and large-group exploration of a topic or theme, is a typical beginning for the initial focus on stereotyping. It might be followed by a student survey on expectations and attitudes toward their adult roles as males and females. (See Chapter 2 for some examples of student responses to such a survey.) These opening strategies can be carried out by the teacher/librarian team in collaboration with a facilitator—from either outside or within a district—who is available to mentor, coach, and consult throughout the school year. (See Chapter 6, pages 82–88.)

Team Planning: Selecting and Implementing a Theme

In meetings during the following weeks, the teacher, librarian, and facilitator focused on selecting and implementing several other lessons designed to explore stereotypes: viewing and discussing a film, values clarification activities, and an exercise analyzing literature. During the facilitator's first planning session with participating staff, both the teacher and the librarian had set long-term goals for the project: helping students read more critically and gain a historical perspective on prejudice in the United States. They had also selected a theme—prejudice/discrimination—which would fit into both the language arts and social studies curriculum.

Matching Themes with Classes

The selection of appropriate themes (and the titles through which the themes will be explored) should involve all members of the collaborative team and should take into account the interests and issues voiced by students as well as the team's goals for the class. One approach when selecting themes is to build on students' past academic experiences. For example, the teacher/librarian team mentioned above selected the theme of prejudice/discrimination in order to follow up on a previous unit on the Holocaust and World War II. Together they identified and examined suitable titles and chose five books: *Journey Home*

(Uchida), a novel about discrimination against a Japanese American family as they return home from an internment camp at the end of World War II; *Alan and Naomi* (Levoy), a story of the developing friendship between a boy from New York City and a girl traumatized by the events of the Nazi occupation of France; *Welcome Home Jellybean* (Shyer), and *Between Friends* (Garrigue), both about the prejudice of children and adults toward young people who are mentally retarded; and *Going Home* (Mohr), in which a Puerto Rican girl from New York experiences discrimination while spending the summer in Puerto Rico.

Another approach to selecting themes is to concentrate on developmental concerns. The theme of families and family relationships spans the interests and developmental needs of young adolescents of different ages. For some eighth grade students, especially girls, family responsibilities become an issue as students find themselves taking on many housekeeping and child-care chores. Reading and discussing such books as *Dicey's Song* (Voigt), *The Friends* (Guy), *Child of the Owl* (Yep), and *Going Home* (Mohr) help students explore the issues related to this theme and their own feelings. A role-play such as "Cheryl and Her Mother," about a girl who disobeys her strict parents, helps students explore the role of the parent, the "good daughter" and the "rebellious daughter," and encourages them to find creative ways to share responsibilities at home.

The theme of families also has great relevance to upper elementary students. One fifth grade class in Project Equal discussed sibling rivalry and parent attitudes at great length. In this heterogeneously grouped class, such books as *The Cartoonist* (Byars) and *Ramona and Her Father* (Cleary) were appropriate for those reading on a fourth grade level. For the more advanced readers, *Charlie Pippin* (Boyd), about a young African American girl who tries to understand her father's preference for her older sister, and *Welcome Home Jellybean* (Shyer) helped students explore the theme through more complex reading experiences. Discussions and writing activities about the ideal family and different family styles helped students become more aware of stereotypes and the realities of American families today. Engaging students in a role-play about attitudes toward sex roles and family chores also enhanced understanding of this theme.

Peer friendship and peer pressure are similarly relevant themes. Many middle and junior high school teachers and librarians see how peer pressure influences adolescents of different ages in such matters as clothing styles, school attendance, and participation in cliques. Many of the books used in Project Equal deal with these issues and allow students to reflect on and discuss them at a distance from their own lives. Such books as *Scorpions* (Myers), *Daphne's Book* (Hahn), *The Friends* (Guy), *Maudie and Me and the Dirty Book* (Miles), and *Shadow Like a Leopard* (Levoy) have characters with whom young adolescent readers can identify. To introduce this theme, teachers might ask students to create a short biography of a real or imagined friend, stressing qualities valued in the friend. While these books are being read, students might also enact role-plays that require decision making in the face of peer pressure.

Drama #3—Cheryl and Her Mother

Cheryl's parents are quite strict with her. They expect her to do well in school and she has a lot of responsibilities at home, like preparing dinner and cleaning up. Her parents both work full-time. Cheryl hardly ever gets to go places with her friends, and her parents won't let her have friends over. Her older brother, Wilson, has tried to convince her to do more with her friends. Finally, Cheryl asks her mother if she can go with her friends to a movie after school, a movie everybody has been talking about. Her mother says no, but at the end of school that day, Cheryl decides to go anyway.

She manages to get home before her mother arrives from work. When her mother gets home, she confronts Cheryl. A co-worker had seen her going into the movie theater, and told her mother. Wilson comes in and tries to support Cheryl.

Characters: Cheryl, Wilson, Mother

What is the problem?

_____

_____

What are some solutions?   Consequences?

1. _____   1. _____

    _____   _____

2. _____   2. _____

    _____   _____

3. _____   3. _____

    _____   _____

If you were Cheryl, what would you do?

If you were the mother, what would you do?

Fig. 2. Role-Playing

Overlapping Themes

Many of the books that highlight the themes of families and peer friendship/ pressure also describe experiences of prejudice and discrimination. A book like *Roll of Thunder, Hear My Cry* (Taylor), narrated by ten-year-old Cassie Logan, shows how the Logan family members support one another and work together to survive. The other major theme running through the book is Cassie's increasing understanding of racism and the fine line between maintaining self-respect and courting danger.

Felita (Mohr) reveals the close, trusting relationship between Felita and her grandmother, as well as her parents' attempt to make a better life for themselves. These themes are set against a backdrop of racial and ethnic prejudice. *Journey Home* (Uchida) and *Jar of Dreams* (Uchida) portray warm, extended families working to build or rebuild their lives together. Both books also show the racism faced by Rinko and Yuki as Japanese Americans in the 1930s and 1940s during the Depression and World War II. *The Gold Cadillac* (Taylor) and *Justin and the Best Biscuits in the World* (Walter) also encompass the themes of family and prejudice. *Alan and Naomi* (Levoy), *The Friends* (Guy), and *Harriet's Daughter* (Philip) combine peer friendship issues with main characters who face prejudice.

Each of these books provides well-rounded stories with interesting, complex characters. Readers can identify with and live through the experiences, good and bad, that the characters go through. While independent reading takes place, students might view and discuss a video of the C.B.S. special, "Names Can Really Hurt Us"[2] or take part in role-plays that explore name calling and exclusion. These activities encourage students to relate the issues and themes in the books to their own lives.

Ongoing Collaboration

Selecting and developing the activities that help bring the themes to life (role-plays, film discussions, and so on) represent another way the teacher/librarian team and facilitator work together. These lessons, which alternate with small group discussions while independent reading continues, should all support the program goals of understanding stereotyping, exploring a theme, and motivating independent reading.

For example, the collaborating team may choose to develop a "Values Line-Up" (see sample) as an activity for the themes of peer pressure and prejudice/discrimination. This lesson requires students to agree or disagree on a continuum from one to five with such statements as, "It is difficult to be close friends with someone of a different race," or "If my friend did something wrong, I wouldn't tell anyone." Numbers from one to five are posted on the walls at intervals around the room, and after completing their written responses, students stand next to the number on the wall representing their opinion. A visual representation or map of the group's opinions emerges. (A large majority may be clustered by number two, for example, with others sprinkled over the remaining numbers.) Several students standing by each number are asked to explain their views. Each explanation adds an insight to the theme.

As the implementation of the selected theme progresses, the librarian, teacher, and facilitator also work together to monitor and assess student reading by considering the following questions: Are the books selected appropriate for the reading and interest level of all the students? Is more time needed to finish the books? Are extra motivational techniques necessary (reading a chapter aloud or asking students to give a book talk on a title they really loved)?

PEER FRIENDSHIP/PEER PRESSURE: Values Line-Up

Check the number for the word or words that best describe how you feel about each
statement.
   1 = Strongly Agree
   2 = Agree
   3 = Undecided
   4 = Disagree
   5 = Strongly Disagree

	1	2	3	4	5
1. It's impossible for boys and girls to be friends with each other.					
2. If my friend did something wrong, I wouldn't tell anyone.					
3. It's difficult to be close friends with someone of a different race.					
4. It's better to go along with the crowd than to be alone.					

Fig. 3. Values Line-Up

The collaborators should also decide how they want students to report on
their reading. Possible formats might include response journals, a notebook of
book summaries, or an art project or book review.

Starting the Reading Process

As soon as the library/teacher/facilitator team is satisfied with its selection of
novels, multiple copies need to be secured so all interested students can read the
book of their choice. Since library media centers seldom have eight to ten copies
of the same title, additional copies of chosen titles might need to be obtained
through special order or borrowed on interlibrary loan.

Book Talks

Introducing the books to the students in a way that creates interest is a vitally important task. Book talks, presented by the library media specialist, the teacher, or a student, are an effective way to begin. A typical book talk lasts about three minutes and reveals just enough of the story line to interest a potential reader. The four rules that follow ensure a successful book talk: (1) Be sure you've read the book; (2) only talk about books you like; (3) never give away the ending; and (4) be brief.

Connecting the book to experiences of potential readers (for example, asking students if they remember how it felt to be the new girl or boy) is especially helpful when giving book talks to reluctant readers. A book talk for *Daphne's Book* (Hahn) might go as follows:

> Seventh grader Jessica is horrified when Mr. O'Brien chooses her to be Daphne's partner in the "Write a Book Contest." Daphne is so weird, she never speaks to anyone and dresses in odd, mismatched clothes. But as the two girls spend time together, Jessica finds a real friend in the mysterious Daphne. She also finds out a tragic secret, and must decide between her loyalty to her new friend and her deep feeling for what is right.

Students should have the opportunity to choose their book immediately after the book talks, if possible. Typically, after hearing enticing talks on books that relate to their own concerns, students rush to select the books, sometimes fighting over popular titles. One participating teacher complained, "I'm in competition with my own students to get and read these books!"

Although the books and lessons in the project are designed to become an integral part of the language arts or reading program, the focus is on reading for pleasure. Experience has shown that giving students the freedom to select their own books is worth putting up with a little temporary confusion and disappointment, and perhaps one or two poor choices. Students can return and exchange books during the one-, two-, or three-week reading period.

Independent reading is enhanced by providing class time for reading and by informal discussions among the teacher, students, and library media specialist about books they are reading. In one school several students ran over to the desk of a teacher during a silent reading period. She had been crying, and they knew she was reading *Bridge to Terabithia* (Paterson). They wanted to tell her that they had cried, too, while reading it, and they proceeded to discuss the book together.

Discussing the Books: The Importance of Questions

Meeting with a small group of students to discuss a book that everyone has read can be one of the most enjoyable and rewarding aspects of a multicultural literature-based program. The discussion or reading response group format involves a group of students and an adult leader participating as active readers. Basing their comments on both the text and personal knowledge, members of the group use the discussion as a forum to articulate and build meaning through prediction, hypothesizing, confirming, and personal sharing. In Project Equal, a successful response group uses questions that help readers uncover new meaning in the book and that enable them to relate incidents and issues in the book to their own lives. The discussion leader listens carefully to the questions student readers raise and accepts alternate meanings.

Questions used for discussion need to be formulated in such a way that students can respond according to their own understanding. The facilitator or discussion leader may then ask the student to clarify the response or ask another student to add to the group's understanding. Positive aspects of group responses to reading have been documented by Golden[3] and Eeds and Wells,[4] whose observations confirmed that small group responses to a text read individually helped clarify and extend the meaning and encouraged a deeper response to the book under discussion. The questions used in Project Equal are designed to explore each book according to the theme selected for focus, such as peer friendship, families, or prejudice. Answering these questions requires taking a careful look at character motivation and specific gender roles and relating these observations to one's own experiences.

Questions that focus on and explore the major theme or themes in a book might be expressed as follows:

"Describe Ramona's feelings about her family. Did she like her family?" (*Ramona and Her Father,* Cleary).
"Now that Felita was twelve, her family treated her differently. How does she feel about this? Why do Mami and Papi treat her brothers differently?" (*Going Home,* Mohr).

Questions that relate inferential reading to the main character's motivation, words, and actions include the following:

"Shaun says, 'I'm your stickball friend, your model airplane friend, but I'm not your friend.' What does he mean? Do you have different kinds of friends?" (*Alan and Naomi,* Levoy).

Other questions examine specific roles portrayed in the book (e.g., gender, parent) and ask students to relate them to their own experiences and/or ideas. For example:

"How does Alfie's mother think a boy should act?" (*The Cartoonist,* Byars).
"Leigh's mother says some men, such as his father, have trouble expressing their real feelings. Do you think this is true?" (*Dear Mr. Henshaw,* Cleary).

Most important are those questions that encourage students to relate their own experiences to those of the characters. For example:

"When Mrs. Sakane felt strong emotion, she would sit right down and write a poem. How do you express strong feelings?" (*Journey Home,* Uchida).

"Do you think Thomas J. and Mr. Mason are right when they say you need lessons or training to say nice things and talk about love?" (*The Pinballs,* Byars).

Although critical reading skills and evaluative comprehension are stressed in this approach, some questions also refer to literal understanding and reporting. A brief synopsis of a book might begin the discussion, followed by round table responses to questions posed by the leader and students.

The Logistics of Book Discussions

The library media center is the perfect setting for small group book discussions. Most centers contain long tables spaced apart from one another and a quiet atmosphere conducive to serious discussion. Moving out of the classroom gives a special emphasis to the activity. When a library media center is small or very crowded, one discussion group might meet in the classroom or in a circle in a quiet section of the corridor.

Discussion groups are composed of students who have completed a particular book. For example, the library media specialist or teacher surveys the students before the book discussion to ascertain how many have read (and finished) each of the books previously introduced on the theme. The teacher and library media specialist will have read and will be prepared to discuss at least one of the books; a facilitator may be present to lead a group; a student may be selected who is willing and able to lead an additional group.

Preparing for Collaboration: Training Workshops

The keys to a successful literature-based program are regular planning meetings and collaboration between teaching team members as they select lessons and books, evaluate, monitor, and plan. Both the collaborative process and the implementation of the curriculum are prepared for through participatory workshops that model team teaching and cooperative library-classroom planning.

Training workshop sessions, held to bring together teacher/library-media-specialist teams from all of the participating schools, provide a "hands-on" look at curriculum activities that the staff will be implementing with their students. They also model collaborative planning among staff members. In Project Equal three all-day training sessions are held off-site before implementation begins. Another model might involve an initial workshop to increase awareness of stereotyping, and then ongoing workshops after the program begins in the schools. Workshops can be led by outside facilitators, district library media coordinators, language arts coordinators, or an experienced teacher/library-media-specialist team.

The initial activity of each workshop is an icebreaker, designed to help establish trust and support and get people moving around and talking to one another. With a small group, "Introductions" can be used, a technique that asks participants to pair up and get to know their partners through such questions as, "What do you enjoy most about being female or male? What do you enjoy the least?" and "What female and male do you admire most and why?" Each member of the pair then introduces the other to the whole group.

Another type of icebreaker is "Who Are These Famous Women?" In this activity, modeled on the game of "Twenty Questions," each participant guesses the identity of the woman of achievement whose picture and biography appear on a placard on his or her back. The participants move around the group, asking one another *yes* or *no* questions, to discover who their famous person is. Playing this game not only helps sensitize participants to the role of women in history, it also models how this activity can be adapted for classroom use.

Day 1: A Closer Look at Stereotypes

The first all-day session focuses on issues in stereotyping, giving staff an opportunity to explore their own attitudes and values regarding gender, racial, ethnic, age, and disability stereotypes. In Project Equal we often encounter the perception that women and people of color have made significant gains over the last three decades in overcoming prejudice and discrimination. To focus teachers and library media specialists on the pervasive problems that still need to be addressed, an "awareness quiz" has proven effective. This quiz, which is not graded and is discussed as a group, questions the test-taker on a knowledge of current statistics about diversity in the workforce, the home, the school, and the publishing world. An example has been provided.

Another effective activity to help participants think about commonly held stereotypes is called "How We See Others." Teachers and library media specialists examine photographs in small groups and brainstorm possible student responses to such questions as "What adjectives might your students use to describe this person? What job or interests might your students associate with this person? Do you see any possible stereotypes in this description?" Photographs include both males and females from different racial/cultural, age, and disability groups. Sample photographs that have been used include a young adolescent boy jumping rope, a woman in a sari working in a laboratory, and an African American woman in a wheelchair holding a protest sign. Participants are asked to honestly evaluate possible student responses and articulate stereotypes they feel their students possess about particular groups.

The purpose of this quiz is to let you check your present knowledge and awareness of some aspects of discrimination and bias in our society. It is meant as an awareness building tool and your score will not be recorded.

Instructions: Please answer the following questions as best you can individually. Then we will discuss the answers as a group.

Fill in the blanks

1. The average median earnings of all women who worked in 1992 were _____ percent of men's earnings.

2. Men's earnings peak at age 55. Women's earnings peak at age _____.

3. African American and Hispanic female workers earn _____ percent of the wages of white male workers.

4. _____ percent of American women work outside the home.

5. _____ percent of women with children under the age of 1 work outside the home.

6. _____ percent of American women working outside the home say they do most of the food shopping, housecleaning, and cooking.

7. For every dollar earned by a white nondisabled male, a black disabled female earns less than _____ cents.

8. Only _____ percent of American families are made up of an employed father, a homemaker mother, and two children.

9. Female students make up _____ percent of the students in New York City's technical/vocational high schools.

10. Over _____ percent of the girls in junior high and high school classes will be engaged in paid employment at some time in their lives and can expect to spend _____ years in the work force.

11. More than _____ percent of children entering the New York City school system at Kindergarten come from homes speaking languages other than English.

12. Although sometimes described as a "model minority," _____ percent of Asian American students in New York City dropped out of school in 1992.

13. Single parent families are underrepresented in basal reading series. Less than _____ percent of the families depicted in basal readers are headed by single parents.

14. Out of every 100 children's fiction books published this year, there will be _____ depicting the African American experience.

15. In 1973 there were 20 children's books published on Puerto Rican themes. How many books featuring Puerto Ricans were published in the early 1980s? _____

Fig. 4. Awareness Quiz

At the conclusion of this workshop, novels used in the program that deal with specific stereotypes are introduced through book talks. Books that might be featured are *Felita* (Mohr), which portrays discrimination against a Puerto Rican family when they move into a new neighborhood; *The Friends* (Guy), the story of a new girl from the Caribbean who is harassed because of her accent and scholarly demeanor; *In the Year of the Boar and Jackie Robinson* (Lord), which features the isolation and acculturation of a Chinese American girl; and *The Gold Cadillac* (Taylor), which depicts an African American family from Ohio experiencing Jim Crow laws on a trip south in the 1950s. All the participants read a novel in preparation for the next training workshop.

Day 2: Developing a Critical Attitude toward Stereotyping in Children's Literature

The second workshop in the series focuses on using children's literature to understand stereotyping and develop critical approaches to reading. The session begins with a values line up to break the ice, refocus participants' attention on stereotypes, and provide a model for an awareness activity that can be used with students (see page 63). Participants are asked to consult their own feelings in several statements on a continuum from one (strongly agree) to five (strongly disagree). Statements might include the following:

It's very difficult to be close friends with someone of a different race.
I don't know how to relate to disabled persons when I meet them face to face.
To be a good parent, you have to subjugate career to family and social needs.

Numbers from one to five are placed at intervals around the room, and respondents are asked to stand on the number that represents their view so that the range and prevalence of opinions becomes visually clear. A follow-up discussion illuminates the range of views.

Another workshop activity that sensitizes participants to possible stereotypes in children's literature and issues of diversity involves the analysis of a brief passage from a juvenile novel or a picture book. After reading the selected passage, participants are asked to reflect on the author's presentation of the character(s), and to compare it with other books about characters from the same background. Some issues to be considered are what adjectives the author has used to describe a family, a male or female character, or a neighborhood; whether or not there are stereotypes in the passage; and how Italian Americans, mothers, Asian Americans, or whatever groups are under study are usually described in children's literature.

Responses can be tallied on a chalkboard and ways of handling a stereotyped passage or character in an otherwise high-quality children's book can be discussed. Helping the staff look at and analyze stereotyped treatments of characters or situations in the context of a historical period or an author's particular

background or perspective models how teachers and library media specialists can work with students to think critically about the books they read. A useful follow-up to this critical analysis activity is a discussion of the criteria used in selecting multicultural fiction as described in Chapter 4.

A major feature of the second training session is modeling how to facilitate a book discussion group using the multicultural novels the students will be reading as part of the literature-based program. A set of questions, adapted for adults and based on the book under discussion, is used as a guideline by the discussion leader.

When there are thirty to forty staff members in the workshop, three or four discussion groups will go on concurrently, each led by an experienced facilitator. The guided questions focus on the themes of prejudice/discrimination, peer pressure, and family, and ask participants to analyze characters and situations in the books for stereotypes. The facilitator models open-ended questioning techniques, eliciting personal responses to the characters and situations, and developing a shared "meaning" of the book.

The developmental appropriateness of these themes for young adolescents is discussed, and book talks are presented to illustrate thematic issues. Linking activities, such as role-playing and writing activities, which both precede and extend the book discussions, are introduced through videotapes, examples of student work, and participatory activities in which a teacher, library media specialist, or principal can "rehearse" possible conflict scenarios.

Day 3: Curriculum Strategies for the Schools

The final day of training involves new participants and a number of experienced Project Equal staff who will share their experiences and expertise with the new people. The session begins with participants meeting in small groups to brainstorm responses to complete the following openers:

1. What I expect from this program . . .
2. What I need from the program . . .
3. What I am concerned about, or fear . . .
4. What I don't want . . .

A recorder in each group lists all responses on chart paper and posts responses on the wall. Participants are then encouraged to walk around the room, reading the comments from other groups.

Once the responses of the total group have been compared and analyzed, participants might come together to hear a speaker or a panel presentation. Popular speakers have included Project Equal book authors from a variety of ethnic and racial backgrounds discussing diversity in children's books and a panel representing nontraditional careers for women. Alternatively, films or videos that relate to stereotyping and prejudice may be viewed and discussed.

The remainder of this final session is devoted to mini-workshops that feature successful units, lessons, or approaches to Project Equal books and themes. These workshops are prepared and facilitated by teachers and library media specialists who have worked with Project Equal staff in implementing the program in their schools. Workshop topics might include: "Expanding the Family Theme: Creating Oral Histories"; "Project Equal Literature: Springboard for Writing Projects"; "Techniques for Motivating Reluctant Readers." New participants have the opportunity to select two mini-workshops based on their interests.

The skills necessary to introduce and maintain a multicultural literature-based program are consistently modeled through participatory activities such as a values line-up, role-playing, and analyzing text for stereotypes. In each of the training sessions, films, videos, posters, and other curriculum materials that might enhance the program are introduced and discussed. Participants begin to develop familiarity with multicultural fiction through book talks and small group book discussions.

Working together for three days with their school partner as well as staff members from other schools and districts helps new participants build trust and support and sets the stage for collaborative program implementation in the schools. Generating and discussing short- and long-term goals and meeting with experienced library-media-specialist/teacher teams through the mini-workshops helps new participants focus on the collaborative process. How are partnerships

What I Am Concerned about or Fear . . .

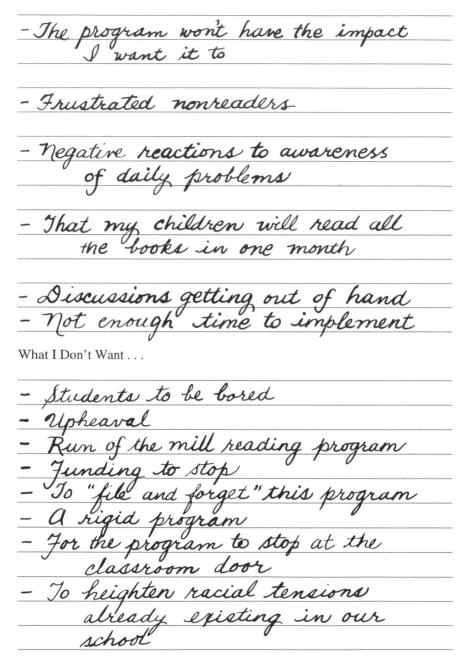

- The program won't have the impact
  I want it to

- Frustrated nonreaders

- Negative reactions to awareness
  of daily problems

- That my children will read all
  the books in one month

- Discussions getting out of hand
- Not enough time to implement

What I Don't Want . . .

- Students to be bored
- Upheaval
- Run of the mill reading program
- Funding to stop
- To "file and forget" this program
- A rigid program
- For the program to stop at the
  classroom door
- To heighten racial tensions
  already existing in our
  school

Fig. 5. Responses to Brain-Storming

What I Expect from the Program . . .

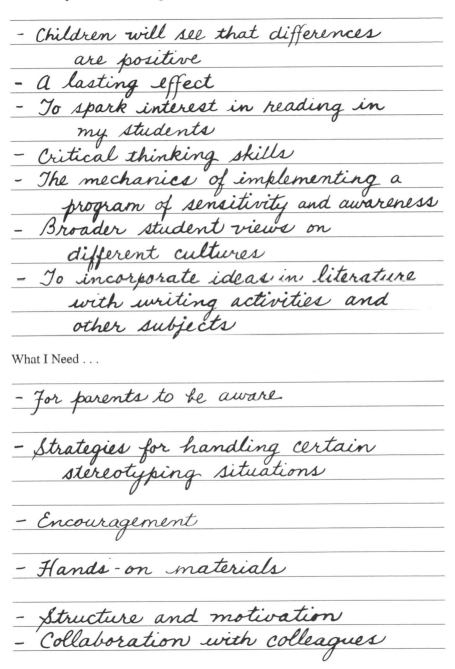

- Children will see that differences
  are positive
- A lasting effect
- To spark interest in reading in
  my students
- Critical thinking skills
- The mechanics of implementing a
  program of sensitivity and awareness
- Broader student views on
  different cultures
- To incorporate ideas in literature
  with writing activities and
  other subjects

What I Need . . .

- For parents to be aware

- Strategies for handling certain
  stereotyping situations

- Encouragement

- Hands-on materials

- Structure and motivation
- Collaboration with colleagues

Fig. 5. Continued

between teachers and library media specialists created and maintained at the school level? Chapter 6 will discuss the conditions necessary for successful collaboration and explore case studies of library-classroom partnerships.

Notes

1. Binnie Meltzer, "A Model of Library-Classroom Collaboration," *Project Equal Newsletter* 1 (Summer/Fall, 1991): 1.

2. Anti-Defamation League of B'nai B'rith, *Names Can Really Hurt Us* (New York: WCBS T.V., 1989).

3. Joanne M. Golden, "Reader-Text Interaction," *Theory into Practice* 25 (Spring 1986); 91–96.

4. Maryann Eeds and Deborah Wells, "Grand Conversations: An Exploration of Meaning Construction in Literature Study Groups," *Research in the Teaching of English* 23 (Feb. 1989): 4–29.

6

Models for Collaboration: Staff Training and Work in the Schools

Collaboration . . . must be taught, learned, nurtured, and supported, until it replaces working privately.

Ann Lieberman, Matthew Miles, and Ellen Saxl
Teacher Leadership: Ideology and Practice[1]

Collaboration between teachers and library media specialists is an integral part of a multicultural literature-based program. Each of the partners brings varied skills and perspectives on teaching diversity and children's literature to the collaborative relationship. How are the conditions necessary for successful partnerships between the classroom and library created and supported? This chapter describes theoretical considerations and specific models of staff development and collaboration developed as part of our program.

One of the roadblocks to collaboration is a long-standing tradition of teacher isolation and the concept of teaching as a private activity. Teachers often have little contact with other adults during the school day, except at lunchtime. Teachers may also feel cut off from one another because of differences in the subject or grade they teach and differences in such personal characteristics as age, gender, and racial or ethnic background. They rarely have the opportunity to come together to discuss the real issues, both theoretical and practical, that concern and sometimes divide them.

Within this tradition, the idea of having someone enter another's classroom to plan, work, and evaluate together may seem threatening and untenable. Critically analyzing another colleague's teaching methods has been particularly off limits. Education has been characterized as an "egalitarian" profession, with differences in good and bad teaching seen as "just a matter of style."[2]

Library media specialists may feel particularly isolated. Frequently the only member of their profession in the school, they have reported to Project Equal that they have no one to talk with who understands their concerns and perspective. If the school district does not have regular meetings and staff development sessions for school library staff, they feel even more alone and have few opportunities to learn new strategies and approaches.

Often there is no time or mechanism for library media specialists to meet with classroom teachers to plan lessons jointly or suggest resource material for classroom curriculum units. Inflexible scheduling, a common practice in New York City at the elementary school level, requires school library media specialists to "cover" the class in the library during the teacher's preparation period. This practice ensures that the teacher will be unavailable for joint planning or team teaching during the library period.

Perhaps because many teachers "drop off" their class at the library door, they have a limited view of the role of the library media specialist as one who just "checks out" books or teaches "library skills" in isolation. Teachers may not see the potential value of working with such specialists in a collaborative relationship.

Establishing a Collaborative Relationship

For successful collaboration to take place in schools, meaningful interaction among participants and a sense of ownership of proposed new ideas are essential. Kulleseid and Strickland speak of the necessity of participants' understanding the nature and purpose of proposed changes, and "internalizing the goals and objectives. They must adapt to new circumstances and simultaneously begin to modify the innovations as they integrate them into their basic professional agendas."[3] Colleagueship will be established as the partners share trust and support. The partners must recognize one another's commitment to the program they are about to undertake. Both must have a similar view of student needs and share long-term goals. They must also understand the day-to-day working of their partner's role as classroom teacher or library media specialist. This shared commitment and understanding will facilitate "buying into" a new program or an innovation, such as a literature program that emphasizes diversity. Once a sense of ownership has been established, the partners can work as a team, problem solving and implementing the program together.

In Project Equal, the process of establishing a collaborative relationship cannot begin until a school or district has "bought into" the program by signing an agreement that establishes the services the program will provide to the schools and commits funding for those services. This process is usually initiated by a district library coordinator, a school library media specialist, or a district or school administrator who has heard about the program while attending a Project Equal workshop or observing in a participating school. A district superintendent or principal might decide to participate in the program because it meets specific district or school objectives, including awareness of multicultural issues, implementing a whole language approach, or fostering interdisciplinary collaboration. Sometimes the program is implemented because of a history of bias-related incidents in a district and the subsequent mandate to deal directly with stereotypes and diversity.

Once the program is in place, project staff meet with the participating administrator and staff in each school to obtain administrative support and cooperation. The real process of library-classroom collaboration begins in the initial off-site training sessions and continues in regularly scheduled consultation and planning meetings in the school. In the off-site workshops, participants and workshop leaders work together to solve problems, share feelings and experiences, and explore values and beliefs. Once the program is established in the schools, the process of working together in the classroom and library begins: co-teaching or sharing aspects of the lessons, planning and evaluating together, and finding time to reflect on personal educational concerns.

What specific elements are needed to develop ownership and create an atmosphere conducive to collaborative change? Lieberman, Miles, and Saxl outline five steps for implementing teacher leadership in a school that can provide a model for instituting a collaborative literature-based program between teachers and library media specialists. The five steps are (1) building trust and support; (2) diagnosing the organization of the school; (3) dealing with process; (4) using resources; (5) building skills and confidence.[4]

Building Trust and Support

An important first step in effecting collaboration and change is to create an atmosphere that encourages feelings of trust and expressions of support among participants and colleagues. A trusting relationship is begun through workshop activities that allow participants and workshop facilitators to work together, solving problems and sharing information, feelings, values, and experiences. Such workshop activities as analyzing photographs for stereotypes, book discussion groups, and brainstorming ask participants to work together in small groups, sharing observations and responding both personally and as educators. The workshop leaders model collaborative teaching throughout the training sessions. While co-presenting, they encourage participant sharing and discussion, and they mediate differences in points of view.

Once the program begins in the school, project participants build on the relationship developed in the workshop series. This process includes co-teaching and meeting together to reflect, develop new strategies, and evaluate. The combination of model teaching and facilitated reflection firmly establishes the trust and support necessary for risk taking and collaboration.

Diagnosing the Organization of the School

A literature-based program such as Project Equal requires examining the school structure to identify how the innovation can be incorporated into the existing school program. On-site planning meetings help the collaborating staff focus on those elements that foster or hinder a smooth and successful implementation.

For example, is scheduling a problem, so that students come into the library only once a month? Are students being pulled out for special programs just as book discussions begin each week? Is the library frequently commandeered for special luncheons or meetings, so that the momentum of the instructional unit is lost? What changes in the school, grade, or class organization need to be made or mediated? Once these problems have been diagnosed, collaborating staff or the facilitator can articulate the needs and benefits of the program to an administrator, dean, or chairperson.

Diagnosing an organization's strengths also helps maximize the chances for success. Strengths present in individual schools, such as a flexible library schedule, parent volunteers, or a television/media center, can and should be incorporated into program planning. Other concerns worthy of diagnostic evaluation might include the impact of grade level or department curriculum goals on lesson planning and the coordination of special programs like visits by a "poet in the school" with literature lessons.

Dealing with Process

Both off-site training sessions and the on-site collaboration in the Project Equal model have been designed to help teachers and library media specialists understand and become a part of the process of working collaboratively and begin to use innovative techniques and new curriculum materials. Each of the activities experienced by participants in the training sessions is based on lessons that will later be used with students. Both the process of working and planning together and the process of developing and successfully implementing lessons are modeled in the training sessions. Once participants and workshop leaders have completed an activity such as role-playing or a "Values Line-up," there is a pause during which everyone can respond to the activity and the rationale and anticipated outcome are described.

A literature-based program and the collaborative process must fit into and yet change the ongoing school curriculum. At the biweekly meetings among the library media specialist, teacher, and program facilitator, much of the talk is practical and focuses on identifying what is happening in the classroom, in the library, and at home when the students read independently. In the meeting, staff decide collaboratively which activities the students will be involved in. Planning includes who will introduce the new lesson, how to relate it to the reading, and who will summarize what has been covered in class at the end of the lesson. The facilitator models techniques both for planning cooperatively and for methods of co-teaching in the library and classroom.

Using Resources

In a collaborative literature-based program, the participating school staff must identify and locate the best resources for successful implementation. Each training session includes a packet of bibliographies, resource lists, and articles on professional issues. Working together, teams of teachers and library media specialists ascertain which books are already in their school libraries and which will need to be ordered. People resources also can be identified. In schools where Project Equal has been implemented over the years, other staff and administrators have participated directly as book discussion leaders and panelists, or have suggested and referred such people as parents and retired teachers who were able to serve as book discussion leaders or as interviewees for research and oral history projects.

Building Skills and Confidence

Workshop activities and on-site support and consultation provide opportunities for practicing specific skills and techniques. Interpersonal skills and techniques for initiating open-ended questioning, facilitating ongoing planning meetings, or developing a staff workshop are modeled and practiced throughout the program. More specific skills, including presenting an interesting book talk, involving students in a role-play, or operating an Ektagraphic camera as part of an oral history project are modeled by the facilitator and can be perfected by the participating staff during the ongoing program. Working together in a supportive environment, participating teachers and library media specialists learn new skills and develop confidence in their abilities.

Partnerships and the Changing Role of the Library Media Specialist

Working in partnership with classroom teachers helps break down isolation and can serve as an important source of colleagueship and support for the school library media specialist. As the perception of the role of the school library media specialist has changed, school practitioners have been encouraged to move beyond the passive "keeper of materials" to active participants in the educational process, working together with teachers planning curriculum and implementing instructional experiences for students.[5] This impetus has come largely from the professional library literature and such national guidelines as *Information Power: Guidelines for School Library Media Programs,*[6] which urge school library media specialists to take the initiative in forming working partnerships with classroom teachers and administrators to design and implement classroom instruction.

The practice of school library media specialists nationally, however, has lagged behind the proposed model. Craver notes that although there has been an increased emphasis on their instructional role in recent professional literature and standards, research studies point to a delay in actual implementation.[7] Hortin also found that few library media specialists do much in the way of instructional development.[8] Part of the difficulty in establishing partnerships between the classroom and the library has been the lack of working models.

One specific plan for collaboration and proactive leadership on the part of the library media specialist is provided by Cleaver and Taylor. Their approach, termed T.I.E., parallels that of the teacher-leader model described by Lieberman, Miles, and Saxl. The three elements of the T.I.E. model are talking (selecting participants and setting up goals, a format, and a trial unit for implementation), involving (identifying resources, assessing needs, and matching these to the unit proposal), and evaluating (collaboratively judging the effectiveness of resources and instructional strategies).[9] A literature-based curriculum and staff development program such as Project Equal can provide a concrete example of how classroom teachers and library media specialists can work together to plan and implement awareness activities, promote independent reading through book talks, discuss and respond to literature in small groups, and conduct such research projects as oral histories in the library media center.

The Benefits of Collaboration

Modeling Diversity

When teachers and library media specialists teach and plan together as colleagues, the collaboration itself models for students and staff the inclusion and acceptance of different perspectives in the classroom and library media center.

For example, in implementing a program that explores stereotyping and attitudes toward race, ethnicity, and gender, it is extremely effective for a teacher-librarian team of different races, ethnic backgrounds, and/or sexes to work together. Such partnerships provide a multicultural context for discussing sensitive issues, sharing both unique and common feelings and experiences, and implementing— as a team—such lessons as a "Values Line-Up" that help students explore the issues. (For an example of this activity, see page 63.) Lee, referring to the impact of interracial collaboration in teaching Black Women's Studies, states that "there is a certain strength of conviction and presence that is generated when there are two models present in pivotal positions in one classroom."[10]

In Project Equal interracial collaboration has proved to be an important model for both students and staff, demonstrating how staff members with different perspectives can discuss diversity and work together. In a junior high that had once been a target for integration but was now predominantly African American, an assistant principal joined the facilitator, the teacher, and the library media specialist during a consultation meeting to discuss the students' responses to a "Values Line-Up" that explored interracial friendships. The staff members present had worked in the school between fifteen and twenty years, and with the facilitator as mediator, the assistant principal, who was African American, and the teacher and librarian, who were white, began to talk about the racial divisions among staff in the school that dated back to an integration attempt years before and to a racially divided teachers' strike. The three admitted that the division was never openly talked about, but that students were aware of the lack of interracial collegiality. They discussed causes and results of this deep division, acknowledging it was a relief to finally talk about the situation and its negative impact on the school.

Both the teacher and the library media specialist described feeling more open in discussions of racial attitudes with students following this meeting (which lasted far beyond the forty-five minutes scheduled for consultation). In the following year, the assistant principal encouraged a newly appointed African American teacher to participate in the program. She and the librarian collaborated successfully, implementing both the literature curriculum and the specific lessons on stereotyping. They also set a modest interracial precedent through their friendly partnership.

This type of collaboration is only possible in racially integrated settings, but the model of multiple adult perspectives in the classroom and the school library media program is important to students even when staff come from similar backgrounds. The teacher and library media specialist bring their own particular professional perspectives and approaches to literature to this partnership.

Modeling Reflective Teaching

Regularly scheduled planning meetings can help teachers and library media specialists become "reflective practitioners," educators who take the time for disciplined inquiry and personal reflection about the issues that arise when implementing a multicultural literature-based program that explores stereotyping. These reflections and discussions, in which adults often relate personally to the themes of peer pressure, prejudice, and family responsibility, translate into a thoughtful and integrated approach to working with children. A few of the issues that have arisen during consultation meetings devoted to implementing a multicultural program are feelings of failure, lack of classroom management skills or administrative support, concerns that race is an issue in professional collegiality or student outcomes, the media's impact on students' self-concepts, and questions about students' lack of independent reading. Without the collaborative environment that fosters these consultations, educators would have been less likely to reflect deeply on such matters.

The Role of the Facilitator

Planning and implementing curriculum changes require leadership and staff development. Someone must act as catalyst and support for these changes. Depending on the circumstances, responsibility may rest with a staff developer or specialist at the building, district, or Central Board level who facilitates the curriculum implementation and staff training. Models that could be appropriate and effective include an outside facilitator who is not connected to the school or the district (as we use in Project Equal), a facilitator from within the school (a position that could be occupied by a teacher, the library media specialist, or an on-site staff developer), or a coordinator from the school district.

The facilitator role combines aspects of mentoring, coaching, and consultation. To be effective, Little suggests, a facilitator, coordinator, or teacher-leader should combine skill training in specific techniques, approaches, and ways of using new materials with whatever assistance or consultation will enable the participating staff to "establish the 'fit' between new ideas and established habits."[11]

The Outside Facilitator

Project Equal uses the model of the outside facilitator in several urban school districts. The project coordinators who developed the curriculum and provide the staff training are housed at the Central Board. Each year they contract with districts and individual schools to train and assist teachers and library media specialists in implementing the program in the schools.

This model has been perceived as an effective one by both the facilitators and the participating schools and districts for several reasons. The facilitators work off-site part of the year and have offices at the Central Board. The time away from the schools provides time to reflect, share ideas and experiences, read new titles, and develop additional areas of curriculum that are responsive to the needs of the schools.

Additionally, working in a number of schools that together represent a range of economic, racial, and ethnic diversity gives outside facilitators a larger and more complex perspective. What books work best with which students? What issues are teachers concerned with in different neighborhoods or school settings? The facilitators can use this information in developing lessons, selecting new books, and in sharing different experiences with students and staff. Recognizing those needs and interests that are common to all students and those that are particular to one school population helps the facilitators be proactive, flexible, and responsive.

From the point of view of staff members participating in the program, an outside facilitator is an objective supporter. The facilitator is there to help them implement the program, not to evaluate them in any way or report back to a district or school administrator. This ability to provide assistance from outside the framework of school or district helps build trust and a sense of collegiality and imparts a vision of change: it has worked in other schools; we can help you make it work here.

School-Based Facilitators: Three Case Studies

A different model is possible in a setting where collaboration, especially between the library media center and classroom, has been ongoing and vital, and where new projects and approaches are implemented routinely. In this setting, where "teachers . . . exert the kind of influence on one another that [enhances] success and satisfaction with students,"[12] library media specialists and teachers implementing a multicultural literature-based program may not need outside facilitation or training. Workshops for other staff members in the school interested in implementing the program can be developed and led by the teacher/library-media-specialist team.

THE LIBRARIAN AS FACILITATOR

The role of the school library media specialist varies from district to district and from elementary to middle school. In situations where the school library media specialists have flexible scheduling, they are in an excellent position to set a model for collaboration and leadership. Classroom teachers often do not work with the school library media specialist to establish reciprocal goals. As Cleaver and Taylor point out, a plan for classroom-library collaboration has not been a part of teacher preservice training or professional guidelines.[13] It is up to the school library media specialist to initiate shared planning and work, and to act as change agent. Even when a school library media specialist has classes scheduled on a regular basis or covers other teachers' classes during their preparation period, aspects of collaboration and leadership are possible.

A school library media specialist in a small elementary school had a flexible schedule and worked with one experienced fifth grade teacher during the first year of Project Equal. She and the teacher had worked together on previous curriculum projects, and they collaborated successfully, with the assistance of the project facilitator who consulted with them as a team twice a month. In the second year of the program, the library position lost its flexible scheduling because of budget constraints. The school library media specialist began providing coverages for teachers. During this year, two new teachers joined the program, one experienced and one new to teaching. The facilitator continued to visit the school, providing assistance and support. However, her visits were less frequent, since this was the school's second year in the program.

The school library media specialist took over the role of facilitating the program for the two newly participating teachers. She arranged for lunchtime meetings in which the three of them discussed those lessons that would be implemented, and determined the thematic focus of the reading. Student progress in reading and in response logs or journal writing (a new initiative in the second year of the program) was shared. She met separately with the inexperienced teacher, providing extra support and feedback. This teacher was unfamiliar with using literature in the reading program and found the use of several different titles confusing at first. The library media specialist also arranged for the new teacher to visit other teachers' classes so that she could observe how independent reading and journal writing could be integrated into her regular program. Through her questions and suggestions, the library media specialist assisted both teachers in understanding the process involved in implementing a successful literature program.

In both the combined and individual meetings the library media specialist provided assistance in teaching specific skills, responding to journals, identifying resources in the library media center, and providing guidance in lesson planning. She supported their efforts through positive feedback and encouragement. At the same time she continued to co-teach with the classroom teachers and project facilitator and lead book discussions with both of the participating fifth grade classes. In this way she remained in close touch with the curriculum and the responses and needs of the students. Her experiences and perceptions of the students' engagement in the program informed her guidance of the two new teachers as she combined the roles of teaching partner and facilitator. A number of successful project units involving ongoing thematic reading were implemented during these two years and provide specific examples of the library-media-specialist/teacher collaboration.

Three elements came together in the middle of a thematic reading unit, at a time when the library media specialist and collaborating teachers were beginning to think about a culminating project. The theme of family had been selected by the team as appropriate to the interests and concerns of the two fifth grade classes, and students were reading and discussing such books as *Ramona and Her Father* (Cleary), *Dear Mr. Henshaw* (Cleary), *A Jar of Dreams* (Uchida), *The Gold Cadillac* (Taylor), and *Felita* (Mohr). At the same time, as a follow-up to the initial lessons on stereotyping, the librarian had suggested showing a videotape she had seen at the training workshop. The students viewed and discussed the tape, *A.M.E.R.I.C.A.N.S.,* in which elementary school children are interviewed and asked to comment on their feelings about prejudice and about feeling "American."[14] The third element was a notice from the school district announcing a district-wide multicultural fair.

At a planning meeting, discussion centered around combining the reading focus and interest in the video in some way that could be featured at the district fair. Many of the students in the class were second-generation Americans, and several children had moved to the United States within the last four years, from Peru, Puerto Rico, Jamaica, and Trinidad. One teacher decided to ask her students to interview family members for an oral history project, incorporating some of the question from *A.M.E.R.I.C.A.N.S.* The school library media specialist and the teacher referred to a unit in the Project Equal curriculum guide, *A Closer Look,*[15] which contained oral history questions for students and ideas on conducting such a project. Together they modified the questions, taking into account the ability level of the fifth grade students, and added several questions on "being American."

The teacher introduced the project to her class and asked students to find a family member or an older friend to interview. Once students had made arrangements to interview someone, the school library media specialist brought small groups of students into the library and worked with them on such interviewing

techniques as using a tape recorder, posing questions, and asking follow-up questions.

As the taped or written oral histories were completed, the teacher reviewed them. To enhance the interviews, some students arranged photographs in albums with captions, while others prepared cardboard displays. Students worked in the library media center, locating maps, photographs, or travel books that illustrated an aspect of the oral history—a map, for example, or a photograph of the city their grandmother had come from, or a historical photo illustrating a vignette from World War II or the World's Fair. In order to coordinate the final versions of the oral history project both the teacher and the school library media specialist met frequently during this period, in addition to the curriculum planning meetings with the other teacher. Each staff member prepared an oral history of a family member, which was shared with the students. Seeing their teacher and school library media specialist involved in the same activities and learning experiences and hearing about their teachers' families added importance to the students' own work.

Before the finished projects went off to the district fair, the school library media specialist hosted a minifair in the library so that all of the upper grade students could have the chance to view, read, and hear the oral histories.

THE DISTRICT FACILITATOR

Another successful model of leadership and collaboration employed in Project Equal schools is the district level facilitator from outside the school. This model closely resembles the Project Equal facilitator role, although district personnel, however involved and invested in using literature and collaborative planning, rarely have time to spend in modeling lessons and co-teaching in schools.

One school district decided to implement the program in several middle schools in an effort to model an integrated multicultural language arts and social studies curriculum. The liaison at the district who initiated the program became the facilitator. She had been involved in bringing innovative language arts approaches to the schools and worked closely with language arts and social studies teachers. She was introduced to the pivotal role of the school library media specialist through the Project Equal workshop series, and she had the opportunity to observe library-classroom collaboration in action when she visited several participating schools.

The district facilitator felt that the methods and lessons she had observed—and participated in at the training workshops—would work well in the upper grades of the district's elementary schools and would fulfill the district's mandate to provide a multicultural focus to elementary school curriculum. Since funding was limited to providing a project facilitator and materials to only middle schools, she set up a series of workshops to train fourth and fifth grade teachers and elementary school library media specialists in aspects of the program. The emphasis in the training session was on the theme of families, and she asked participating teachers to develop a literature unit based on the books used by Project Equal. She visited each school three or four times over the four months allotted to the unit, meeting with the teachers and the library media specialist at each site, providing ideas and support.

The district had a history of active parental involvement. To extend this involvement to include the literature emphasis, the facilitator designed a brief series of parent-child evening workshops. Students shared their reading with parents, and during the workshop sessions wrote and illustrated, with photographs and drawings, their own family stories.

The facilitator continued to join planning meetings and observe project lessons at the middle schools. She provided support for the program by coordinating scheduling and special services between the schools and the district level. In one school she was able to work with the administration to eliminate the use of the library as a homeroom and to obtain funding and time for the library media specialist to order books to improve his fiction and nonfiction collection. In another school that had a television studio, she arranged for media center staff to work with students and project staff to design and film videotapes based on student responses to reading.

In this particular middle school, the teacher and library media specialist had a history of collaborating on language arts and social studies units. In the semester before they began participating in Project Equal, they had worked together implementing a unit on the Holocaust that involved reading historical fiction and biography and interviewing older relatives about this historical period. When introduced to the program, they decided to continue with the theme of discrimination. With the assistance of the facilitator, they selected such titles as *Alan and Naomi* (Levoy), *Going Home* (Mohr), *The Real Me* (Miles), and *Journey Home* (Uchida), which focused on this theme. While independent reading and small group discussions took place, the library media specialist worked with small groups of students finding photographs, posters, and book covers that highlighted the theme of prejudice and discrimination for Black History Month and Women's History Month. The students designed a bulletin board for each month and arranged a display of appropriate biographies in the library. The school library media specialist had a particular interest in history and added several additional titles of historical fiction to the titles students were reading and discussing, including *Shabanu, Daughter of the Wind* (Staples).

Working together during a regularly scheduled once-a-week meeting time, the teacher and the library media specialist wrote discussion questions for these titles and developed lessons that linked these books and such others as *Journey Home* (Uchida), *A Jar of Dreams* (Uchida), and *Child of the Owl* (Yep) to the social studies curriculum. They continued to lead small group discussions of the books and implemented lessons on stereotyping through co-teaching in the classroom and the library. Because of their long-standing working relationship and the perception in the school that the school library media specialist was proactive and knowledgeable, productive collaboration enhanced curriculum planning and access to resources.

THE ON-SITE STAFF DEVELOPER

In several of the schools participating in the program, a staff developer who worked with the language arts or reading curriculum participated in the training sessions and returned to the school in the role of program facilitator. In one elementary school, the on-site staff developer, whose function combined aspects of assistant principal and teacher mentor, was interested in implementing the program and had as a goal more effective working relationships and collaboration among staff members. A lack of responsiveness on the part of the administration to scheduling flexibility and professional enrichment had led to a feeling of disaffection and a practice of noncooperation among the teaching staff. This staff developer perceived that the collaborative model provided by Project Equal could help bring about change in staff practice.

In initial planning meetings, the participating teacher and the library media specialist found it difficult to come to agreement on a theme or general direction; they spoke to the facilitator or the staff developer but not to each other. Conversations were stilted and there was a tendency to use the meeting time to air complaints about general conditions in the school. One cause for friction was the perception that the library media specialist had more preparation time than other staff members. The staff developer mediated the planning meetings, focusing conversation on setting goals for the program and looking at student interests and reading tastes. She arranged for the library media specialist to give a presentation on the resources of the library at a staff conference, and she worked with teachers on each grade level to make sure all classes were scheduled into the library on a regular basis.

She also set up a weekly meeting time for the school library media specialist and the Project Equal teacher to review the students' reading journals and evaluate the progress of the program. The two staff members responded positively to the support and "fair" treatment provided by the staff developer; improved dialogue allowed them to focus energies on the program and on working together to implement various aspects of the curriculum. The collaborative model required by the program provided the impetus for the first step toward change.

Does an innovative approach to multicultural fiction and collaborative library-classroom partnerships work over the long term? This question is addressed in the concluding chapter, in which evaluation data and anecdotal reports from Project Equal participants (students and staff) are discussed. Case studies of successful implementation and conditions necessary for the success and maintenance of the program are examined as guides to replicating the program in other school settings.

Notes

1. Ann Lieberman, Matthew Miles, and Ellen Saxl, "Teacher Leadership: Ideology and Practice," in *Building a Professional Culture in the Schools,* ed. Ann Lieberman (New York: Teachers College Press, 1988), 156.

2. Judith Warren Little, "Assessing the Prospects for Teacher Leadership," in *Building a Professional Culture in the Schools,* ed. Ann Lieberman (New York: Teachers College Press, 1988), 78–106.

3. Eleanor R. Kulleseid and Dorothy S. Strickland, *Literature, Literacy, and Learning* (Chicago: American Library Association, 1989), 33.

4. Lieberman, Miles, and Saxl, "Teacher Leadership: Ideology and Practice," 153.

5. Kathleen W. Craver, "The Changing Instructional Role of the High School Library Media Specialist: 1950–84, *School Library Media Quarterly* 14 (Summer 1986): 183–191.

6. American Association of School Librarians and Association for Education Communications and Technology, *Information Power: Guidelines for School Library Media Programs* (Chicago: American Library Association; Washington, D.C.: Association for Educational Communications and Technology, 1988).

7. Craver, 190.

8. John A. Hortin, "The Changing Role of the School Media Specialist," *TechTrends* 30 (Sept. 1985): 20–21.

9. Betty P. Cleaver and William D. Taylor, *The Instructional Consultant Role of the School Library Media Specialist* (Chicago: American Library Association, 1989).

10. Valerie Lee, "Strategies for Teaching Black Women's Literature in a White Cultural Context, *SAGE* 6 (Summer 1989): 74–75.

11. Little, "Assessing the Prospects for Teacher Leadership," 86.

12. Ibid., 81.

13. Cleaver and Taylor, "The Instructional Consultant Role of the School Library Media Specialist," 11.

14. Steven Okazaki, *A.M.E.R.I.C.A.N.S.* (Los Angeles: Churchill Films, 1980).

15. Lauri Johnson and Sally Smith, *A Closer Look: An Interdisciplinary Approach to Stereotyping* (Brooklyn: New York City Board of Education, 1988).

Reference

Staples, Suzanne Fisher. *Shabanu, Daughter of the Wind.* New York: Knopf, 1989.

7

Long-Term Results of a Multicultural Literature-Based Program

In addition to promoting team planning and a cooperative effort, [Project Equal] introduced the students to non-stereotyped roles in society. It opened up a world of exciting children's literature, which we hope will serve as a foundation for life-long reading and learning.

> Louise Miller, Lucille Lerner
> Middle School Librarians
> I.S. 125Q[1]

What have we learned after working with teachers, library media specialists, and students over the last eleven years in a multicultural literature-based program? Have teachers integrated more multicultural literature into their reading program? Do library media specialists establish partnerships with teachers to motivate reading for pleasure? Are students more aware of issues of stereotyping and diversity and more critical readers? What elements sustain successful collaborative partnerships between teachers and library media specialists over the long term?

Every year Project Equal participants complete a written evaluation, assessing the strengths and weaknesses of the program and how they and their students have been affected by it. These results over the last eleven years consistently show that teachers and library media specialists have incorporated new teaching methods, modified their literature selection techniques, implemented strategies to motivate reading for pleasure, and established collaborative partnerships with other staff members. Significantly, staff members report that they themselves have become more aware of stereotyping in literature and society and more sensitive to issues of diversity as a result of participation in the program.

Adopting New Teaching Methods

Working with other adults in a literature-based program not only breaks down the isolation experienced by school staff, it also provides ongoing models of such teaching techniques as open-ended questioning, small group book discussions, and role-playing. Project Equal participants consistently rate in-class support as the most effective aspect of the program. The project facilitator initially models new methods. As the program progresses, the teacher and library media specialist begin to team teach alongside the facilitator, practicing new teaching methods in a supportive environment. Modeling becomes a non-threatening way to pass along new techniques. In the words of a language arts teacher, the facilitator "participated actively in my school for the first two years of the program, and I was able to model my future lessons after those which were so ably demonstrated."

Open-Ended Questioning

In Project Equal open-ended questioning is initially utilized in class discussions to help students become aware of the concept of stereotyping and to clarify their own attitudes and values toward issues of diversity. Some teachers and library media specialists report that this is the first time in their professional careers that they have engaged in class discussions that are not aimed at arriving at the "right answer." They acknowledge feeling more "relaxed" in discussions, "listening" more to their students, and becoming more accepting of student opinions.

Book Discussions

Small group book discussions are often mentioned as one of the most effective new approaches that teachers and library media specialists learn in Project Equal. One library media specialist stated that this program increased her awareness of how to engage in a "dialogue" with students about literature, instead of the usual adult-centered monologue. Other teachers and library media specialists reported that they had begun to use the book discussion techniques with other children's literature.

Role-Playing

Role-playing scenarios depicting peer pressure and family conflicts, often derived from incidents in the books used in Project Equal, is a novel and somewhat threatening proposition for many teachers and library media specialists. Staff are afraid they will lose "control" of the class or that they might be uncomfortable with the students' responses. Having another teaching adult who "models" this technique helps teachers and librarians "try it out" in a safe atmosphere. After witnessing this technique at the second training workshop, one library media specialist approached the project facilitator and stated that "she was sure that role-playing was one approach to literature she didn't want to try." The project facilitator reassured her that her school didn't have to use role-playing if she didn't want to. About three months into the implementation of the project, she was sufficiently comfortable with the program that she approached the project facilitator again. "Let's try role-playing. I'll follow your lead." She became an active proponent of role-playing problem situations, working with the language arts teacher to dramatize scenes from the novels and discuss possible solutions with the students.

Developing and Refining Selection Guidelines

By exploring the concept of stereotyping and reading and discussing multicultural fiction that emphasized diversity, teachers and library media specialists report becoming more aware of racism, sexism, and developmental issues in children's literature for young adolescents. "The books chosen for the program were highly motivating and dealt with issues that are really on the minds of young people," stated one teacher. Selection criteria is initially discussed in the training workshops, but questions of why one book was included and not another continue to arise periodically during biweekly planning meetings.

The process of discussing stereotypical characterizations with students helped teachers and library media specialists refine their own selection criteria. "I find I am more selective in the books I choose for use in the classroom," said one teacher. Another teacher/library-media-specialist team reported that they were "trying to find more books that relate to the students' backgrounds" as a result of participation in Project Equal. A multicultural literature-based program can help staff view children's literature in a new light. "Our Project Equal liaison assisted us in developing a unique way of evaluating and applying the literature the children were reading," acknowledged one library media specialist.

Motivating Reading for Pleasure

Teachers and library media specialists found that their students read more through the use of motivational techniques such as booktalks, access to multiple copies of popular paperbacks, and opportunities to share responses to novels through small group discussions, art projects, and journal writing. "My class read more books this year than they ever read before and enjoyed reading more," stated one teacher. "Even the poor readers were stimulated into reading by the motivational techniques used in Project Equal," commented a library media specialist. A special education teacher was particularly enthusiastic. "Our students look forward to reading! They were thrilled to read as many books as they have, and look forward to reading more over the summer."

A key element in increasing reading for pleasure for many classroom teachers was allowing students to choose which Project Equal novels they would read. In the words of one classroom teacher, "I'm much freer with allowing them to choose their own materials, drop unsatisfactory ones and pick up others—as a result, they are actually reading *more.*"

Opening Minds to Diversity

A literature-based program that emphasizes diversity sanctions the discussion of such real life problems as prejudice and discrimination, peer pressure, and family relationships as an integral part of the school curriculum. "Through the use of selected literature they [the students] were able to understand and deal with racial, ethnic, and sexual differences and stereotypes," stated one staff member.

By discussing multicultural literature with students, the school staff found they, too, became more comfortable dealing with issues of diversity that arose in the classroom or school environment. One teacher mentioned that she was "better able to handle sensitive topics and discussions in a nonjudgmental way" as a result of her involvement in Project Equal. The presence of other teaching adults in a collaborative relationship helped reassure some participants that they would have assistance in discussing controversial issues. "Some of the delicate topics we discussed in Project Equal I might not have done without the support of the program," admitted one participant. Other teachers and library media specialists reported that they spent more time discussing values with the students.

Many teachers and library media specialists found that they themselves became more aware of stereotyping as a result of participating in Project Equal. One teacher stated, "I used to stereotype without realizing it. . . . I'm not so quick to make generalizations now." Another teacher mentioned that "after nineteen years I have found an exciting program which *I* enjoyed. My students tell me I stereotype less."

What Students Learned

During the first eight years of the program, surveys were administered to participating students before and after the program to assess its impact on their perceptions of gender roles and the amount of independent reading students did. Highlights of the major findings were

> In general, most students enjoyed the project and learned what the program aimed to teach. For example, students mentioned recognizing stereotypes and prejudiced characters in the books they read, and described feelings of empathy and understanding for the characters in the novels.
>
> Students who participated in the project became less gender specific in their perceptions of appropriate activities and careers for males and females than those in a comparable group not involved in the project. For example, students wrote about resenting stereotyping and being able to look at roles for men and women more objectively.
>
> The change in sex role attitudes to include more nonstereotyped responses was greater for younger students (fifth and sixth graders) and for girls than for boys.

All students read more as a result of the program, but on the average, girls engaged in more independent reading than did boys.

Younger students (fifth and sixth graders) engaged in more independent reading than did older students (seventh and eighth graders).[2]

The evaluation surveys assessed student attitudes only toward gender roles. As the focus of the program changed to include racial and ethnic stereotyping, an increase in the number of participating schools and the lack of funds and staff made it impossible to continue the formal evaluation of student attitudes. In addition, the lack of validated evaluation tools to assess adolescents' racial and ethnic attitudes precluded a formal examination, although anecdotal evidence indicates many students were more aware of racial prejudice and discrimination as a result of participation in Project Equal.

Impact on Independent Reading

One interesting finding was that girls engaged in more independent reading than boys. Although the difference was not great, it held true at every grade level and was more pronounced with older students. One explanation could be that boys see reading in general as a "feminine" activity, as some researchers have suggested.[3] Our surveys in Project Equal over the years have not supported this notion. Boys and girls have consistently rated reading as an activity for both sexes, including reading novels.

Another explanation may be that Project Equal emphasizes realistic fiction, while some of the research on reading interests indicates that older boys prefer nonfiction, particularly informational books on sports and science by male authors.[4] In other words, realistic fiction that focused on family and peer relationships may have proved more interesting to the girls, resulting in more independent reading.

Occasionally seventh and eighth grade boys have complained about the limits of the Project Equal collection, particularly requesting more books with male protagonists. In fact, many middle school teachers report that the Project Equal books that feature male coming-of-age stories, such as *Scorpions* (Myers) and *Shadow Like a Leopard* (Levoy) were the first books some of the boys in their classes had completed on their own. We try to be sensitive to this issue and continue to search for multicultural fiction with male protagonists that depicts a variety of gender roles and family styles.

An additional finding indicated that younger students (fifth and sixth graders) as a whole engaged in more independent reading than seventh and eighth graders. This result may be related to structural and philosophical differences in language arts programs at the elementary and junior high level. The project books often became the major focus of the language arts program in the fifth and sixth grades at the elementary school level. Writing assignments and surveys from the Project Equal curriculum were implemented in place of previous assignments and lessons. Self-contained classes and a flexible elementary reading program enabled fifth and sixth grade teachers to adopt the Project Equal book list and thematic reading approach during at least one semester of their language arts curriculum.

Even in elementary schools that had departmentalized reading, the classroom teacher participating in the program was likely to use multiple copies of the project books for his or her reading group, and to recommend appropriate project titles to remedial teachers. The same was true of sixth grade language arts teachers at the middle school level who had self-contained classes.

Elementary classroom teachers had oversight regarding students' work, and they integrated the language arts curriculum holistically, so that independent reading was not interrupted by term papers or other assignments. In seventh and eighth grades, however, students had a different teacher and a more regulated syllabus for each subject, creating a setting in which independent reading was affected in two ways. One was, simply, less time to read for pleasure in school and at home. Typically, each major subject required homework every night and the teacher did not provide reading time in school. A second way this setting limited independent reading was that the mandated language arts curriculum required students to study a genre of literature in a specific format, usually involving all students reading the same novel such as *The Pearl* (Steinbeck) or *The Outsiders* (Hinton) and, upon analyzing and completing that genre, moving on to another.

The majority of middle school and junior high language arts teachers participating in Project Equal did implement a thematic approach, using selected novels. Some teachers had been organizing student reading around themes already. However, many language arts teachers only worked with their seventh and eighth grade classes for a forty-five minute period three or four times a week. Less student contact time also limited independent reading, making it difficult to introduce more than one or two themes with the older students during the term.

Connecting Reading and Real Life

In addition to the formal evaluation, which took place from 1981 to 1988, library media specialists and teachers over the years have asked their students to write about what they learned from the books and activities they engaged in through Project Equal. Students independently made the connection between reading and real life issues. Writing about the book *Felita* (Mohr), a fifth grader said, ". . . just by reading that book you can see that Project Equal teaches you much more than just how to read." A seventh grader admitted, "I feel that some of the project books I have read have reminded me of some of my friends and even my family in certain ways. It has cleared up some things—that I thought I was different, but am not so different."

Learning to Collaborate—Teachers and Library Media Specialists Working Together

What has been the long-term impact of partnerships between teachers and library media specialists in a multicultural literature-based program? In examining teacher/library-media-specialist teams implementing Project Equal, we have seen that in general the most important elements for ongoing collaboration have been positive interpersonal relationships and the experience of success in the program. Sharing similar goals and teaching styles and feeling comfortable with one another and the curriculum proved extremely important in the day-to-day collaboration. Sometimes successful teaching partners were also friends, eating lunch together and even socializing outside of work. Often, they were just sympathetic colleagues open to working together in a fairly low-risk situation.

Although administrative support was helpful, it was not always an essential element in a successful collaboration. Selecting compatible team partners, however, was critical. In general, when librarians were consulted in the selection of a language arts or classroom teacher, they chose someone with whom they knew they could work. Often, previous successful collaboration was the basis of the choice. Occasionally, successful library-classroom partnerships in other subject areas proved not to be a good measure by which to predict successful collaboration in a literature program that focuses on stereotypes and issues of diversity.

Five Case Studies of Successful Collaboration

Specifically, in our eleven years with Project Equal, we have learned that successful collaborations—a key to the success of the program itself—are more likely to occur if a participant (1) seeks a partner who is open to diversity; (2) focuses on genuine personal interests and strengths; (3) works to establish equality within the partnership; (4) adopts a proactive stance, often leading the effort when needed; and (5) responds to the needs of both students and staff. The case studies that follow highlight the importance of each of these elements of successful long-term collaboration.

CASE #1: FIND A PARTNER OPEN TO DIVERSITY

An experienced library media specialist in a middle school selected a language arts teacher she had worked with successfully on Shakespeare projects for many years. As a participant in Project Equal, however, the teacher had a great deal of difficulty accepting student choice in reading for pleasure and the validity of reading realistic contemporary fiction, particularly novels written in African American English. This teacher also refused to participate in open-ended discussions of sex role surveys and values clarification techniques that ask students and staff to explore their views of family roles and peer pressure. It came as a surprise to the librarian that the colleague who shared her love of Shakespeare would feel so differently about issues of diversity.

Although the library media specialist and teacher continued to work together on other projects, in the second year of Project Equal the library media specialist selected a teacher with a more humanistic, problem-solving approach to the middle school language arts curriculum. When the project facilitator visited the school three years later, the library media specialist and the second teacher were still working together and implementing selected aspects of the program. The library media specialist had ordered replacement copies of the most popular titles, and several of the books on the themes of peer pressure and discrimination had been integrated into the language arts curriculum. Role-plays and surveys on peer issues were also still being used. The teacher and library media specialist developed additional curriculum units, including one in which students wrote poems featuring characters and situations from the books.

CASE #2: FOCUS ON YOUR INTERESTS AND STRENGTHS

In a second middle school, the library media specialist was particularly skillful at developing and involving students and staff in special programs as a follow-up to research projects. Two of her largest and most successful programs, a Women's History Month assembly and a panel on nontraditional careers, evolved from her participation in Project Equal and her close collaboration with several language arts teachers. She sought out teachers over the years whom she recognized as dynamic and interested in issues of equality, as well as supportive of the use of literature in the classroom. She set up weekly meetings and had definite goals for the implementation of the program. This library media specialist also had a clear sense of what would and would not work in her school setting. Once the project facilitator was no longer making on-site visits, the library media specialist continued to implement thematic reading, small group book discussions, and research projects in collaboration with two or three language arts teachers who shared her interest in women's history and equality issues.

CASE #3: CREATE AN EQUAL PARTNERSHIP

A library media specialist, new to a third middle school, initiated collaborative projects and lessons with teachers from many departments in the school. The school climate did not support collegiality, however, and after the first year, only a handful of teachers continued to express interest in maintaining a curricular partnership. The librarian enlisted a committed language arts teacher to work with Project Equal. The first two years of the program, supported by visits by the project facilitator, were very successful. Independent reading, small group discussions, and end-of-term projects focused on prejudice and discrimination, a topic of concern to both the staff and administration of the school. In addition to sharing these concerns, the library media specialist and teacher, although different in background and personality, shared common goals for the students and similar teaching styles; these commonalities, as well as a similar level of commitment, helped create an equal partnership.

In the following years, the library media specialist and teacher continued to work with the language arts teacher's sixth grade classes, and the library media specialist developed units that examined racial discrimination based on the study of such books as *Journey to Jo'burg* (Naidoo), *The Gold Cadillac* (Taylor), and *Felita* (Mohr). She also successfully involved a special education teacher and her students in the lessons and small group discussions. Attempts to involve two additional language arts teachers were less successful. The library media specialist attributed the problems in ongoing collaboration to differences in teaching styles, approaches to classroom management, and the teachers' failure to support independent reading and to follow up literature-based lessons in the classroom.

CASE #4: BE PROACTIVE

A middle school library media specialist who was particularly successful at maintaining independent reading and small group discussions worked with several different language arts teachers over the years. She contacted the teachers, set up planning meetings to discuss collaborative implementation, and arranged her schedule to accommodate small groups from participating classes to discuss the books. Project Equal helped her move from an isolated position in the library to a proactive force in the school, involving many members of the language arts department and enhancing the reading program.

CASE #5: BE RESPONSIVE TO STUDENT AND STAFF NEEDS

Choosing teachers to collaborate on Project Equal in an elementary school setting is sometimes difficult, because the program involves only fifth and sixth grade classes and many elementary schools now end at the fifth grade. This limitation often leaves the library media specialist and principal with a choice among only three or four teachers. Despite this problem, a successful model of long-term partnerships and program implementation occurred in a small elementary school where a dynamic library media specialist who also functioned as part-time grant writer for the school put her knowledge of the school's needs to work in getting the program established. She was very effective at assessing student and staff needs and bringing innovative programs into the school to meet those needs. She recognized that Project Equal would promote a literature-based approach to reading and provide a model for students and staff to discuss and understand diversity and prejudice in society. As a former teacher in the school, the library media specialist had first-hand knowledge of the strengths of the teaching staff and which upper grade teachers might be open to the program.

Over several years, she worked with four different teachers. She ordered extra copies of multicultural fiction used in the program so that all of the classes in a grade could be involved in thematic reading. She also used some of the simpler titles with younger children, adapting curriculum lessons based on the books. By the time she left the school, a thematic approach to literature and many of the lessons on stereotyping from Project Equal were an integral part of the fifth and sixth grade curriculum. Her position was filled by a teacher who had also participated in Project Equal and who continues to work with new teachers to implement a multicultural literature-based program.

Problems with Collaboration

Although the rewards of working collaboratively are great for both students and practitioners, implementing a curriculum that requires active collaboration can be problematic. Over the years of implementing Project Equal, teachers, library media specialists, and project facilitators have identified five areas of difficulty: interpersonal relations, different teaching styles, inflexible scheduling, the perception of the role of the library media specialist, and school climate.

INTERPERSONAL CONFLICT

The description of the collaboration mediated by the staff developer mentioned in Chapter 6 is a good example of interpersonal conflict that can threaten the success of the program. In this situation, an on-site staff developer, working intensively with uncooperative staff, effected change. Another solution would be for the library media specialist to choose a teacher with whom she or he has a good working relationship. When an administrator agrees to implement and pilot new programs in the school, it is in the school's interest to allow the staff to select the programs and partners they want to work with.

DIVERSE TEACHING STYLES

Different teaching styles are not always apparent until two staff members begin to work together. Some staff members may not be comfortable talking about diversity or implementing learner-centered teaching techniques such as open-ended questioning, role-playing, or small group book discussions. It may be helpful to first present the idea of a multicultural literature-based program in a faculty or department meeting. Teachers who are interested in the concept can volunteer as team members.

INFLEXIBLE SCHEDULING

Inflexible scheduling, more common in elementary school libraries than middle school or junior high libraries, generally means a class is scheduled into the library once a week during the teacher's preparation period. In this type of scheduling pattern, the library media specialist rarely has free periods in which individual students or small groups of students can come to the library to browse, engage in independent research, or work on special projects. For a multicultural literature-based project to work successfully, the students involved in the program must have regular access to the library. In addition, the teacher and librarian should meet with the class together at least once a week in the library to conduct book discussions.

The ideal, of course, is to have a flexible library schedule that allows the librarian to schedule classes into the library on a "need" basis in consultation with the classroom teacher. If this is not possible, the class or classes participating in a multicultural literature-based program must be able to schedule at least one period a week in the library when both the library media specialist and the teacher are available to work with the students.

In Project Equal, we have found that administrators can rearrange schedules if they realize that the success of the program depends on the school staff's having time for team teaching and joint planning. In some cases, successful collaboration between the classroom teacher and the library media specialist in Project Equal convinced principals of the educational value of collaboration and resulted in restoring flexible scheduling in the library media center program.

LIMITED PERCEPTIONS OF THE LIBRARY MEDIA SPECIALIST'S ROLE

Differing perceptions of the role of the school library media specialist continue to make it difficult to establish partnerships between classroom teachers and librarians. Although Schon, Helmstadter, and Robinson found that principals and library staff in Arizona were largely in agreement about what the role of the library media specialist should be,[5] we have found that school staff and administrators at the elementary and middle school level in New York City often have divergent views of what librarians "do." Library media specialists complain that they are not included in departmental curriculum meetings or consulted about resources for special projects. Given the narrow view that many classroom teachers hold of the librarian as the "person who checks out books," the impetus must come from the library media specialist to be proactive and advocate classroom-library collaboration. Library staff who have initiated Project Equal in their schools have been able to expand classroom teachers' perceptions of the importance of the library in the school through a successful example of a classroom-library partnership.

INHOSPITABLE SCHOOL CLIMATE

Sometimes the overall school climate is so chaotic or the school staff so demoralized that innovation and collaboration not only goes unnurtured but may be actively sabotaged. In some schools, teachers are encouraged by their colleagues not to take on extra projects or develop innovative curriculum because it challenges the status quo. School staff may be resentful of a rigid or unsupportive administration and feel that the only way to register their dissatisfaction is by resisting special projects. Library-classroom partnerships cannot flourish in this type of atmosphere. Problems with the general school climate, often related to an unresponsive administration and a lack of trust and support among staff, must first be addressed before trying to institute a multicultural literature-based program.

Sustaining Innovation and Collaborative Partnerships

How does a teacher/library-media-specialist team continue their partnership over the long term without the presence of a facilitator to nurture the collaboration and provide outside resources? In examining long-term partnerships between school staff involved in Project Equal, we have identified certain strategies that have helped sustain the program and keep the partnerships going over the years.

MAKE THE PROGRAM YOUR OWN

Teacher/library-media-specialist teams who have continued to implement Project Equal for several years after their initial training have incorporated selected aspects of the program into their ongoing curriculum. Some teams focus on encouraging students to read multicultural fiction independently and conduct occasional small group book discussions. Other staff have incorporated role-playing into their language arts curriculum, having students problem-solve conflict scenarios based on the books they are reading and act out solutions. One library media specialist uses such women's history activities as researching and portraying "living biographies" of women of achievement with all her library classes. Another librarian focuses on exploring oral histories and family traditions with her largely immigrant student population.

To sustain an innovative program that emphasizes issues of diversity in literature and society, library media specialists and teachers must be responsive to their students and implement those aspects of the program that are most appropriate to their teaching styles and setting.

SHARE YOUR SUCCESSES

Periodically we invite experienced participants to attend a "reunion" workshop to review the latest multicultural fiction and share their successful collaborations and strategies for keeping a multicultural literature program going on their own. Providing a forum for teacher/librarian teams to present joint projects recognizes the expertise and professionalism of practitioners and helps break down the isolation "school people" often feel. An informal network is created in a district as library media specialists and teachers talk at the workshop and sometimes make arrangements to visit other schools.

A newsletter provides another forum to share successes. Project Equal publishes a newsletter once a year with information about projects that were implemented in schools that participated in the program that year. This newsletter is also distributed to schools that are no longer officially in Project Equal but continue to implement aspects of the program on their own.

CREATE A COOPERATIVE CLIMATE IN THE CLASSROOM AND LIBRARY

Teachers and library media specialists are transformed and energized when they approach a multicultural literature-based program as a joint learning venture with their students. Reading and discussing literature together that speaks to young adolescents' need to make sense of their lives is deeply engaging for both students and staff. Sharing personal responses to multicultural fiction models for students an openness to diversity and a critical approach to literature. Working together with colleagues to select literature, develop lessons, and implement a library-classroom curriculum overcomes isolation and provides a supportive environment for risktaking. When students and staff deal with diversity and read critically together, everyone learns and grows.

Notes

1. Louise Miller and Lucille Lerner to Geraldine Clark, 17 June 1987.
2, Lauri Johnson and Sally Smith, *Summary of Evaluation Results—Project Equal—1981–1988* (Brooklyn: New York City Public Schools, 1990).
3. Hilary Taylor Holbrook, "Sex Differences in Reading: Nature or Nurture?" *Journal of Reading* 31 (March 1988): 574–576.
4. Deborah Langerman, "Books and Boys: Gender Preferences and Book Selection," *School Library Journal* 36 (March 1990): 132–136.
5. Isabel Schon, Gerald C. Helmstadter, and Dan Robinson, "The Role of School Library Media Specialists," *School Library Media Quarterly* 19 (Summer 1991): 228–233.

References

Hinton, S. E. *The Outsiders.* New York: Dell, 1968.
Steinbeck, John. *The Pearl.* New York: Penguin, 1986.

Project Equal Fiction
Book List—1992–1993

Families

Boyd, Candy Dawson. *Charlie Pippin*. New York: Puffin, 1988
Byars, Betsy. *The Cartoonist*. New York: Puffin, 1987.
———. *The Pinballs*. New York: Harper Trophy, 1987.
Choi, Sook Nyul. *Year of Impossible Goodbyes*. Boston: Houghton Mifflin, 1991.
Cleary, Beverly. *Dear Mr. Henshaw*. New York: Dell, 1984.
———. *Ramona and Her Father*. New York: Avon Camelot, 1990.
———. *Ramona and Her Mother*. New York: Dell, 1988.
———. *Strider*. New York: Morrow, 1991.
Garza, Carmen Lomas. *Family Pictures/Cuadros de familia*. San Francisco: Children's
     Book Press, 1990.
Herzig, Alison Cragin and Jane Lawrence Mali. *Sam and the Moon Queen*. New York:
     Clarion Books, 1990.
Myers, Walter Dean. *Won't Know Till I Get There*. New York: Puffin, 1988.
Paterson, Katherine. *The Great Gilly Hopkins*. New York: Harper Trophy, 1987.
Shyer, Marlene Fanta. *Welcome Home Jellybean*. New York: Alladin, 1988.
Voigt, Cynthia. *Dicey's Song*. New York: Ballantine, 1984.
Walter, Mildred Pitts. *Justin and the Best Biscuits in the World*. New York: Knopf, 1991.

Peer Friendship/Peer Pressure

Boyd, Candy Dawson. *Forever Friends*. New York: Puffin Books, 1986.
Garrigue, Sheila. *Between Friends*. New York: Scholastic, 1978.
Guy, Rosa. *The Friends*. New York: Pocket Books, 1980.
Hahn, Mary Downing. *Daphne's Book*. New York: Bantam, 1985.
Hansen, Joyce. *The Gift Giver*. New York: Clarion, 1980.
———. *Yellow Bird and Me*. New York: Clarion, 1986.
Levoy, Myron. *Alan and Naomi*. New York: Harper Trophy, 1987.
———. *Shadow Like a Leopard*. New York: Harper & Row, 1981.
Mathis, Sharon Bell. *Sidewalk Story*. New York: Puffin, 1986.
Miles, Betty. *Maudie and Me and the Dirty Book*. New York: Bullseye (Knopf), 1980.
Myers, Walter Dean. *Scorpions*. New York: Harper Trophy, 1990.
Paterson, Katherine. *Bridge to Terabithia*. New York: Harper Trophy, 1987.
Philip, Marlene Nourbese. *Harriet's Daughter*. Toronto: The Women's Press, 1988.

Prejudice/Discrimination

Cohen, Barbara. *Molly's Pilgrim.* New York: Bantam, 1990.
Hansen, Joyce. *Out from This Place.* New York: Walker, 1988.
―――. *Which Way Freedom.* New York: Walker, 1986.
Hurmence, Belinda. *A Girl Called Boy.* New York: Clarion, 1982.
Lord, Betty Bao. *In the Year of the Boar and Jackie Robinson.* New York: Harper Trophy, 1986.
Miles, Betty. *The Real Me.* New York: Bullseye (Knopf), 1989.
Mohr, Nicholasa. *Felita.* New York: Bantam, 1990.
Naidoo, Beverly. *Chain of Fire.* New York: J. P. Lippincott, 1989.
―――. *Journey to Jo'burg.* New York: Harper Trophy, 1988.
Sadiq, Nazneen. *Camels Can Make You Homesick.* Toronto: James Lorimer, 1985.
Taylor, Mildred D. *The Gold Cadillac.* New York: Dial, 1987.
―――. *Roll of Thunder, Hear My Cry.* New York: Puffin, 1991.
Uchida, Yoshiko. *A Jar of Dreams.* New York: Alladin, 1985.
―――. *Journey Home.* New York: Atheneum, 1978.
―――. *Journey to Topaz.* Berkeley, Calif.: Creative Arts Book Co., 1985.
Yee, Paul. *Tales from Gold Mountain.* New York: Macmillan, 1989.

Self-Awareness

Cisneros, Sandra. *The House on Mango Street.* New York: Vintage, 1989.
Mohr, Nicholasa. *Going Home.* New York: Bantam, 1989.
―――. *Nilda.* Houston: Arte Publico, 1986.
Myers, Walter Dean. *Fallen Angels.* New York: Scholastic, 1988.
Paek, Min. *Aekyung's Dream.* San Francisco: Children's Book Press, 1988.
Smucker, Barbara. *Runaway to Freedom.* New York: Harper Trophy, 1978.
Soto, Gary. *Taking Sides.* New York: Harcourt Brace Jovanovich, 1991.
Yarbrough, Camille. *The Shimmershine Queens.* New York: Bullseye (Knopf), 1990.
Yep, Laurence. *Child of the Owl.* New York: Harper Trophy, 1990.

Author/Title Index

Lauri Johnson has graduate degrees in reading and curriculum development and a background in community-based educational programs. She developed multi-cultural educational programs for women prisoners and ex-offenders in Oregon and has taught reading and special education at the elementary and middle school levels in Oregon and New York.

Sally Smith has graduate degrees in education and administration and a background in children's literature and training pre- and in-service teachers. She is the author of *A Notebook on Planning and Curriculum for After School Programs.*

Ms. Johnson and Ms. Smith developed and coordinate Project Equal, a multi-cultural literature-based program that seeks to create an awareness of stereotyping and critical reading skills. They are the co-authors of the curriculum guide *A Closer Look: An Interdisciplinary Approach to Stereotyping.* The authors received the Whitney-Carnegie Award from the American Library Association to research and compile a comprehensive bibliography on U.S. and Canadian multicultural fiction.

The paper used in this publication meets the minimum requirements of American National Standard for Information Sciences—Permanence of Paper for Printed Library Materials, ANSI Z39.48-1984. ∞

Project Editor: Carol Skinner

Text designed by Peter Broeksmit

Composed by Charles Bozett in Times Roman using QuarkXPress

Printed on 50-pound Finch Opaque, a pH-neutral stock, and bound in 10-point C1S cover stock by McNaughton & Gunn